Chile Pepper Book

The
CHILE PEPPER
BOOK
a fiesta of
fiery, flavorful recipes

Susan Belsinger and Carolyn Dille

 INTERWEAVE PRESS

THE CHILE PEPPER BOOK
by Susan Belsinger and Carolyn Dille

Design, Susan Wasinger, Signorella Graphic Arts
Photography, Joe Coca, except as follows: pages 29 and 31, Susan Belsinger
Photo styling, Linda Ligon
Production, Marc McCoy Owens

Interweave Press, Inc.
201 East Fourth Street
Loveland, Colorado 80537
USA

printed in Hong Kong by Sing Cheong

Library of Congress Cataloging-in-Publication Data

Dille, Carolyn..
        The chile pepper book : a fiesta of flavorful recipes / Carolyn
    Dille and Susan Belsinger.
            p.   cm.
        Includes bibliographical references and index.
        ISBN 0-934026-93-9 : $9.95
        1. Cookery (Hot peppers)   2. Hot peppers.   3. Cookery (Peppers)
    4. Peppers.   I. Belsinger, Susan.   II. Title.
    TX 803.P46D55 1994
    641.6'384--dc20   92-48866
                                                  CIP

First printing: IWP—40M:194:CC

DEDICATION

This book is for Linda Ligon and Joe Coca,

our editor and photographer,

happy chileheads whose good humor and good ideas

are a pleasure to work with.

ACKNOWLEDGEMENTS

Our families and friends are by now used to our fact-finding and photo shoot trips, and to tasting and eating our recipes during development. We are deeply grateful for their continued good humor, patience, and love throughout the work of making this book. Special thanks to Lucie and Cady, who were brave about saying goodbye to Susan. The world of chiles is a large one, with many people who have dedicated their professional lives to sorting through the many mysteries of capsicums. Of these, we would especially like to thank two for their help and interest in our work over the years. Jean Andrews, whose books hold a place of honor in our chile collections, has been gracious and good-natured in sharing information with us. And Jeanne Croft at the University of New Mexico, Las Cruces, has introduced us to wonderful people and places, and likes a chile chuckle as much as we do. We are very glad to have Barbara Ciletti and Gail Jones at Interweave Press working with us. Their enthusiasm and hard work have smoothed and energized our mission to share our love and knowledge of chiles with a wider audience. In the orchestration of a book, many people and processes are involved. We are fortunate indeed that Susan Wasinger of Signorella Graphic Arts designed this one, bringing all the elements together in such a beautiful final form.

TABLE OF CONTENTS

page 9

CHILES
AROUND THE WORLD

page 19

CHILES
IN THE KITCHEN

page 28

CHILES
IN THE GARDEN

page 39

APPETIZERS AND
FIRST COURSES

page 47

SAUCES

page 53

MAIN COURSES

page 65

VEGETABLES
AND SALADS

page 73

SALSAS AND
ACCOMPANIMENTS

page 87

DESSERTS

A profusion of fresh chile peppers.

CHILES AROUND THE WORLD

What is it about chile peppers that inspires such passion among so many peoples around the world? For nearly twenty years we have been collecting answers to this question: on our plates, in our gardens, in books and journals, and among the many chile lovers, growers, users, and scholars we have encountered in our travels. Some people love chiles at first bite; for some they're an acquired passion. But we've found that to know them well is to love them more; we invite you to become better acquainted.

Peppers belong to one of the premier food families of the plant kingdom, the Solanaceae, and count among their cousins such universal favorites as potatoes, tomatoes, and eggplants. Their genus, *Capsicum,* stands out, though, for its large number of species and varieties (hundreds), its many shapes and sizes, its profusion of glossy and attractive colors, and its range of flavor. While flavor varies from apple to apple, thyme to thyme, peppers have a remarkable diversity: sweet to searingly pungent, hot and sweet at the same time, green and vegetal, earthy, and fruity. As Jean Andrews, artist, writer, and pepper lover, describes her own introduction to the pepper family many years ago: "I soon began to look upon the colorful pepper pod as the sea shell of the plant kingdom with its myriad forms, multicolors, exciting textures, and on top of that a pugnacious personality . . . . When you bite one, it bites back."

Like beans, corn, and avocados, peppers are New World plants of considerable antiquity. Pepper remains have been carbon-dated to 7000 B.C. at archaeological sites in southeastern Mexico. Fossilized pepper fruits that are larger than indigenous wild varieties have been dated to 2500 B.C. in northern Peru, suggesting that they were cultivated. This general region, including central Bolivia, is where some experts hypothesize that peppers originated.

Like most New World cultural history, the chile peppers' story has come to us in tantalizing bits and pieces. Some of the ancient peoples who used peppers were preliterate. Others, particularly the Aztecs and Mayas, who gave many chiles the names they still carry today, suffered the misfortune of having their cultural records and monuments destroyed by European invaders.

During the fifteenth century, Columbus was one of a number of European explorers who sought to find sea routes to India, home of black pepper (*Piper nigrum*), then the most expensive spice in the world. Though disappointed that he had not reached India, where he could have filled his holds with the highly profitable spice, he recognized the pungent qualities of the chile peppers he did find. Chiles were totally new plants for the Europeans, and some set about recording their uses and cultivation from the native peoples, collecting seeds, and somewhat later, plants.

Names and Navigations

The Spanish created some confusion of nomenclature by calling the new plants *pimiento*, the same common name of the time for black pepper. But plant taxonomy was in a ferment for some time, and the genus of peppers has been classified and reclassified as *Pimenta, Piper,* and *Capsicum* several times. The French botanist Tournefort selected *Capsicum* in 1700, it's not clear whether from the Latin *capsa* for "box" or "chest" (referring to the seeds enclosed in the fruit) or from the Greek *kapto* for "to bite" (referring to the fruits' pungency). Peppers themselves contribute to the confusion, being prolific and hybridizing easily. Further, chile peppers have many regional and local common names in their homelands and adopted lands. Sometimes a given pepper will be called by different names, according to the town—even the hillside—where it is grown, and whether it is used fresh or dried.

The spelling of the names of different kinds of hot peppers, even of the word "chile" itself, has yet to be codified. In fact, it can stir heated debate and was the subject of a formal declaration, read by Senator Pete Domenici of New Mexico into the *Congressional Record* in 1983. New Mexico, which accounts for more chile pepper production than any other state, prefers "chile". This is the Spanish form of *chilli,* a term the Spaniards took from the Nahuatl language of the Aztecs. Hot peppers are called *ají* in many parts of Central and South America, another term the Spanish appropriated, this from *axi* of the Arawak people indigenous to the West Indies. In this book, we use the words "chile(s)", "chile pepper(s)", and "hot pepper(s)" interchangeably. We use "chili", an American spelling, only to denote the popular stew or the powdered chile and spice blend that is used to flavor it.

Also contributing to the multitudes of names

which chiles have been given is the virtually instantaneous acceptance that they gained around the world after their discovery by European explorers. Between 1493 and 1600, capsicums had journeyed by sea and land to Spain, Italy, Germany, the Balkans, Moravia, Africa, India, and the Far East. Originally spread by the seafaring Portuguese and Spanish, peppers were avidly cultivated and consumed by peoples of many races and cultures from Nagasaki to Canton, Macao, Manila, the Moluccas, New Guinea, Goa, Mombasa, Mozambique, and Cape Town. Overland and sea traders—Arabs, Chinese, Hindus, Persians— carried them throughout the Indian subcontinent and the Middle East, as well as to the islands of Southeast Asia.

There are any number of reasons why chiles were so readily adopted by so many: their flavor, the brightness they contributed to bland diets, their ease of cultivation, the inexpensive alternative they afforded to spices. Even in Europe, where other New World plants, such as the tomato and potato, had a fitful history before they were considered safe and pleasant to eat, peppers became established quickly.

"Revolutionary" is not too strong a word; chiles immediately conquered the palates of the poorest classes, those with the most entrenched food traditions— and this before radio, television, or print advertising. Hot peppers became so thoroughly naturalized in the lands to which they were imported that in 1542, less than fifty years after their introduction in India, some were brought to Europe and labeled by a German professor as "Calicut peppers" native to India. Chile peppers struck a chord that resounded, and still resounds, in the cultural lives and foods of many people.

BETWEEN 1493 AND 1600, CAPSICUMS HAD JOURNEYED BY SEA AND LAND TO SPAIN, ITALY, GERMANY, THE BALKANS, MORAVIA, AFRICA, INDIA, AND THE FAR EAST.

CHILE POWER AND CHILI POWDER

In the United States today, chile power is on the rise, and not just as food. It is producing fan clubs, books, magazines, t-shirts, boxer shorts, aprons, and even a popular rock group. Decorative ristras (ropes of dried chiles) and wreaths are an industry in themselves. An increasing interest in ethnic cuisines has meant that there are more kinds of chiles, fresh and dried, and more chile preparations available in more markets than even five years ago. Consumers can choose Thai and other Asian peppers; chipotles, de árbols, guajillos from Mexico; habanero, Scotch bonnet, and other peppers from Yucatán and the Caribbean.

Commercial salsas have overtaken ketchup as the most common American condiment. Many have names and intensities that appeal to the growing market of lovers of *really* hot pepper: Hellfire and Damnation; Hell in a Bottle Hot Sauce; Mrs. Dog's Dangerously Hot Pepper Sauce; Little Freddy's Hot Lava. Though most of these sauces do not have warning labels to keep out of reach of children, they should. The tingling tongues, ringing ears, and runny noses that accompany bliss among adult chile fans bring tears to those with tender young palates.

This late-blooming love of chiles north of the Mexican border is an historical anomoly. According to current evidence, the capsicums did not grow very far north of the Rio Grande until the Spanish took them there during their northward conquest of what is now the southwestern United States. If, in fact, the native Pueblo peoples of southern Colorado, northern New Mexico, and Arizona did not have chiles before the Spaniards came, they began to cultivate them quickly and enthusiastically. Today chiles, with corn, beans, and squash, are part of the quaternity of traditional Pueblo foods, ones that still inform people's everyday diets, planting and harvesting rhythms, rituals, and celebrations.

On the other hand, Americans of European descent who began to move into the Southwest in large numbers after the Mexican-American War in the mid-nineteenth century were rather slow to realize the sensual appeal of chile peppers. In general, the closer their occupations were to agriculture, and the easier they were in exchanges with native people who crossed the border to work for them, the more quickly they took to chile dishes. By now, several generations of European-descended Arizonans, Californians, Coloradans, New Mexicans, and Texans have grown up eating chiles frequently and happily.

Chile peppers figure in much older stories in their native lands. Pre-Columbian artifacts found in Peru and throughout Central America and Mexico show that peppers played a large role in the civilizations there. Different kinds of chile pods are represented on carved granite obelisks, pottery, and cloth embroidery dating from A.D. 400 to 1400. Pepper bushes and their leaves and fruit are ingeniously worked into motifs that range from mythical creatures to animals, birds, and insects of the region, from tribute piles of peppers presented to royalty, to farmers harvesting peppers. The Mayas, Aztecs, and Incas offered peppers to their gods, often personified in their kings and queens.

Those who have spent any time in chile-producing lands, from the early Spaniards to present-day visitors, are impressed by the number of kinds and varied uses of peppers. Most of the

A collection of colorful capsicums—
Cayenne, Firecracker pequín, Jalapeño, Serrano, Tabasco,
and Thai—in varying hues of ripeness.

ways in which they are processed have been known for hundreds, if not thousands, of years. The Arawak people of the Caribbean pressed the juice from fresh peppers. All of the peoples who ate chiles before Columbus arrived used them fresh and whole, fresh and chopped with other ingredients, fresh and roasted, dried as whole pods, and dried and ground. It seems reasonable to us that they also combined ground chiles with herbs and spices to flavor dishes as we do today with chili powder.

Chili powder was created about a hundred years ago in the United States. It depends on dried chiles, enhanced principally by cumin seed and oregano, occasionally by black pepper, dehydrated garlic, and/or onions. Its inventor was either De-Witt Clinton Pendery or William Gebhardt, depending on the historian you read. Both men immigrated to Texas in the latter half of the

nineteenth century, became interested in Texas dishes and seasonings, and both had chili powders for sale by 1890. Their products were pure, unadulterated with the salt, anticaking agents, or flour that characterize many modern blends. Both men made mild claims about the healthfulness and digestibility of the chiles they used. Though their markets were mainly in Texas and the Southwest, both were successful, and their powders, whose formulas are closely guarded secrets, are still produced today.

During and after the Second World War, chili powder began to turn up more and more often in home and and restaurant cooking, a "secret ingredient" of homemade and commercial sauces and beverages. Through their war travels within the country and abroad, numbers of Americans acquired a taste for the flavors that chiles, herbs, and

spices brought to food.

Aiding this spicy circulation was the McIlhenny family of Louisiana, who had been producing their very hot and famous Tabasco Pepper Sauce since 1868. Tireless promoters of their sauce and exacting in quality control, they were already exporting it to London by 1870. Tabasco Pepper Sauce (a trade-mark name and a patented formula) was originally named for the peppers a friend and neighbor of the founding Mr. McIlhenny brought back with him from the Mexican state of Tabasco. The sauce has kept its curious connection with war, being with Kitchener in Africa and with American forces in the Vietnam and Gulf wars.

Louisianans rival Southwesterners and Texans in love of chiles, and they have developed an abundance of their own sauces and complex chile and spice blends. Louisiana-style hot sauces typically contain only pure pepper juice and/or pulp, vinegar, and salt. The tabasco is the only pepper that produces juice when squeezed with simple pressure. (For an intense pepper experience, squeeze a drop of juice from a ripe tabasco onto the tip of your tongue.) Cajun and Creole chile-spice mixes have a lower proportion of chile to other ingredients than chili powders, but the peppers are quite fiery.

Collective pepper mania has generated its own vocabulary ("chilehead" for those addicted to peppers) and other silliness (members of The International Connoisseurs of Green and Red Chile, an educational-promotional organization, wear handmade fabric Pod Caps in the shape of chiles, and call their president the "Queso Grande"), and an increasing interest in the history, ethnobotany, medicinal value, and cultivation of chiles—not to mention their edible qualities.

PEPPERS, PLEASURE, AND PAIN

Peppers are the only foodstuff that can provoke both intense pleasure and pain. Moreover, they can be addictive, not only for humans, but for chimpanzees, rats, moose, goats, dogs, and chickens, as shown in laboratory experiments and by observation. That they are is the study of psychologists, food historians, anthropologists; the nature of this addiction is the work of chemists and medical researchers.

The compound responsible for both pleasure and pain in chiles is capsaicin, a complex of about a dozen vanillyl amides. Capsaicin is extremely powerful; it can be detected by the human tongue in a solution of a million parts of base liquid to one part capsaicin. The work of extracting and

FOR AN INTENSE PEPPER EXPERIENCE, SQUEEZE A DROP OF JUICE FROM A RIPE TABASCO ONTO THE TIP OF YOUR TONGUE.

measuring capsaicin was done at the turn of the century by a Detroit pharmacist, Wilbur Scoville, who called his system the Scoville Organoleptic Test. His method, which depended on the use of human testers to concur on the number of "Scoville units" in a particular chile (ranging from 0 for bell peppers to 350,000 for habaneros), was the standard for growers, chile processors, and pharmacists until the development of a high pressure liquid chromatography test in the past decade. The latter method, while requiring very expensive equipment, is accurate and reliable; it does away with the need for human testers, who become tolerant of capsaicin, unable to distinguish its intensity after a few tests.

This tolerance is part of the puzzle of pleasure, pain, and pepper addiction. Eating hot peppers triggers a dramatic response in most people—tearing, sweating, and other signs of distress—yet millions of people choose to repeat the experience daily. How to explain it? According to a theory advanced by the psychologist Paul Rozin and described by Amal Naj in his fine book, *Peppers: A Story of Hot Pursuits,* when capsaicin touches nerve endings in the mouth, pain messages are transmitted to the brain just as they would be in an actual burn. These signal the brain to secrete endorphins, natural painkillers that in excess produces euphoria. Each bite of pepper sends another message of pain, provoking another jolt of endorphins. The overall effect is a pleasurable sensation that pepper devotees come to crave.

Another theory, proposed to Naj by Elisabeth Rozin, a food historian, is that capsaicin somehow increases the mouth's sensitivity. As a result, food seems more flavorful. This theory runs counter to the widely held opinion that eating hot peppers dulls one's sense of taste. In fact, regular pepper eaters become more aware of flavor nuances in chiles.

Capsaicin affects different body tissues in different ways. The same people who eat hot chiles with apparent pleasure can experience lingering pain when their fingertips, where many nerve endings are located, touch the capsaicin-rich membrane while preparing chiles. We have both experienced memorable chile burns on our hands: once by not wanting to make a trip to the store for rubber gloves while we were canning jalapeños, another time while preparing two pounds of habaneros for jelly, even though we were wearing thin surgical gloves.

"Hot hands" is also a common affliction among tabasco pepper pickers; tabascos must be picked ripe, but break easily, releasing their capsaicin-rich juice. The mucous membranes of

Habanero and Scotch bonnet are among the hottest chiles. Rocatillo is comparatively mild.

the eyes, nose, and lips likewise are apparently affected by capsaicin so intensely that no release of endorphins is not enough to overcome the burning sensation. In fact, in strong concentrations it can be debilitating, which is why it is the principal component of certain anti-aggressor sprays.

The skin in other areas and the muscles are affected in yet other ways, as native healers in Central and South American have known for centuries and European and North American doctors and pharmacists for many years. Neuroscientists believe that when a concentrated solution of capsaicin is rubbed on the skin, the resulting burning sensation causes pain messengers (Substance P) to notify the brain to start producing endorphins, as described earlier. However, on the skin, capsaicin apparently destroys the Substance P that is attracted to the site.

The body sends more Substance P, and the capsaicin destroys it as well. Finally, when the supply of Substance P is exhausted, the burning sensation ceases. Liniments such as Heet work on this principle, and capsaicin is the active ingredient of creams for painful skin and nerve conditions including shingles and neuralgia. It is being tested in cream form for diabetic neuropathy (which causes burning pain on the bottom of the feet), osteoarthritis, and rheumatoid arthritis.

However capsaicin may mitigate or cause pain, it is a certainty that peppers bring pleasure to about one-fourth of the world's people, some 1,300,000,000 happy chile consumers. They are one of a handful of foods—along with garlic, onions, and other members of the allium family—whose ancient dietary use is proving the wisdom of the ages.

CHILES IN THE KITCHEN

VITAMINS AND VARIETIES

Fresh chiles—gleaming gold, neon orange, scarlet and crimson, chartreuse and forest green, eggplant and lavender purple; round, oblong, arrow- and heart-shaped, large and small—look as if they ought to contribute to our happiness and health, and they do. Not only do they tingle our tongues and stimulate the release of endorphins, they contain large amounts of vitamins C and A. By weight, fresh peppers have about three times as much vitamin C as oranges, limes, and lemons; fresh red chiles have as much vitamin A as carrots. In chile-loving cultures, people get ample amounts of these vitamins, as well as vitamins E and P and potassium, by consuming chiles, both fresh and dried, frequently.

Though nutritive value is roughly the same for all capsicums, from the hottest habanero to the mildest bell, they vary greatly in flavor and heat. And varietal names aren't much help to the cook because they're used so inconsistently. The best way to distinguish chiles is by their shape, color, and flavor. There is some variation in these, but once you have a good idea what a poblano looks and tastes like, you can buy it for chile rellenos whether it is marketed as ancho (which is actually the dried form of poblano) or pasilla (a very different chile in shape and flavor). Farmers' markets are good places for chile recognition experiments. Peppers are still sold by an initially bewildering variety of names, but they are inexpensive, so you can buy a few of several kinds, and take them home to look at them and taste them well. In any market, look at the pepper and not the label. We have prepared a chart (pages 34–38) to help identify the chiles in this book.

The best time to sample chiles is during August, September, and October, when pepper harvests are in progress throughout the country. In other months, most peppers in the market are imported, and you'll have to pick through them to find the freshest. Chiles should be very glossy, completely unwrinkled, and free of soft, black, or bruised spots. Stems should be green, not brown or black, and unwithered. Flavor and pungency, as well as vitamin content, diminish as peppers are kept in storage. Most varieties of really fresh peppers from the garden or farmers' market will keep in a loose plastic bag in the vegetable storage section of the refrigerator for about a week before they start to lose their shine and crispness.

PUNGENCY AND PROTECTION

All the chiles used in this book (and many others, not yet widely available) are pungent to some degree. Whether a pepper is pungent is determined by a gene that controls the production of capsaicin. The degree of pungency is influenced by several factors. The most important is maturity; though capsaicin is present at the beginning of fruit development, it increases as chiles mature. Air and soil temperature and type of soil also influence pungency. Dry, hot climates, where temperatures hardly drop at night, produce the hottest chiles. Though the role of soil nutrients on capsaicin hasn't been fully studied, chiles seem to grow best and be most pungent in loamy soil with plenty of nitrogen, potash, and calcium. Some studies have shown that chiles from the sunny side of plants contain more capsaicin. About 90 percent of the capsaicin is concentrated in the white membranes of chiles; the remainder is found in the seeds and inner walls. Flavor and aroma compounds, which make it possible to distinguish between a serrano and a habanero blindfolded, are located in the outer wall.

To please your own palate and those for whom you cook, we recommend that you taste chiles before adding them to a dish. Individual peppers vary in pungency, and the only sure way to judge a pepper's heat is by tasting. A method we've found useful is to cut off the stem end and run your finger over the flesh that is attached to it. Touch your finger to your tongue, and you will know if it is hot. If it doesn't

IN GENERAL, THE

SMALLER A PEPPER, THE

HOTTER IT IS.

seem hot, touch the flesh to the tip of your tongue, or take a cautious bite with your teeth and tongue, not your lips. Of course, this is easier to do when you grow your own peppers. Many commercial producers, particularly of jalapeños and serranos, market strains that have reduced capsaicin. When we buy chiles from a supermarket, we buy double or triple the amount we would use of garden chiles so that we can add more if necessary. To our tongues, nothing is duller than a salsa without some fire.

What is "some fire" to some is inedible to others. That's why we always describe the intensity of chile pepper dishes to those who will be eating them, even to our families, who have much experience with them. Those whose mouths are burning can find relief by consuming milk, yogurt, or sour cream. These contain ample casein, a protein that cracks the bond between capsaicin and pain receptors.

There are some rules of thumb for pepper pungency. In general, the smaller a pepper, the hotter it is. The main exception to this is the habanero, the hottest pepper known, quite large when compared to a tabasco or tepín. In general, fresh chiles lose some heat when cooked; dried peppers intensify in heat when cooked. Also, some varieties, particularly Thai peppers and fresh tabascos, stay hot in the mouth longer than others. In contrast, habaneros, which have many times the capsaicin of any other chile, sting fiercely but fade quickly.

Always wear rubber gloves when working with chiles. This is the most important advice we can give about working with chiles, and we speak from experience. A capsaicin burn gives a slightly different sensation than a heat burn, and it does not blister, but it can last for a day or two and be extremely uncomfortable. We have tried not wearing gloves and then removing the capsaicin from our hands with vinegar, salt, or a mild bleach solution, but found these minimally helpful, if at all. Although the outside of chiles does not contain capsaicin, bruised chiles and those without stems may have leaked some, and it is easily transferred from cut peppers to skin. Take care not to touch your skin, eyes, lips, or nose until you have removed the gloves and washed your hands thoroughly with soap and water. Thin surgical gloves are fine for working with small amounts of peppers. For large amounts, the slightly heavier disposable gloves usually sold in hardware stores are better. In a pinch, dishwashing gloves will protect you, though they do not have the fit and flexibility for fine knife work.

Cooking Fresh Chiles

Most thick-fleshed peppers have a thin, tough skin that is best removed for pleasant eating. Fresh New Mexico green chiles, Anaheims, poblanos, mulatos, and the sweet bells have this skin. The traditional way of removing the skin is to roast the peppers enough to loosen it. Though· the peppers blacken to some degree, depending on how you roast them, the aim is to blister the skin, rather than cook the peppers through.

We roast peppers any one of three ways, according to the number of peppers we are working with. In every case, we first cut a small slit at the stem end of the chiles to prevent their bursting. For a few chiles, the open flame of a gas stovetop works well. Lay the chiles directly on the burner grates; watch them carefully and turn them frequently with tongs. Wear rubber gloves, in case interior juices containing capsaicin

are exuded. For a larger number of chiles, we place them on a shallow baking pan and set it about 4 inches under the oven broiler. Turn frequently to blister the chiles evenly; watch carefully that they do not cook too much. Even when a section of chile skin is not black, if it wrinkles when pushed with tongs, the chile has been blistered enough. When we have a large harvest, and/or have the grill lit, outdoor grilling is an excellent alternative, blistering the chiles quickly and giving them a bit of smoky flavor. In this method, too, watch the chiles carefully and turn them frequently.

Transfer the roasted chiles to a paper or heavy plastic bag, or wrap them loosely in foil to steam the skins loose. When the chiles are cool enough to handle, remove the skins, seeds, and stem if necessary. For stuffed chile dishes, it is nice to leave the stems on, as they look handsome and are a visual

reminder that the chiles are fresh, not canned.

Working on the paper bag we have used to steam the chiles in keeps our cutting boards free of chile juice, skins, and seeds. Begin by loosening the skin at the stem where you made the slit. When the skin is loosened all around the stem, scrape it down with the flat of a knife, turning the pepper as you scrape. To prepare a chile for stuffing, enlarge the slit to within half an inch from the pointed end. Cut the seed membrane free just under the stem and along the inner walls. The flavor is better when chiles are not rinsed; don't worry about a few seeds or blackened bits of skin. If you are not stuffing the chiles, it is easier to cut the seed membrane and stem together, though you lose a little chile flesh that way.

Now the chiles are ready for any number of tasty preparations: they can be stuffed, diced, or cut into

A trio of spicy salsas: Green Tomato; Habanero, Tomatillo, and Orange; and Mango.

strips. Because the chiles have been partially cooked, they need little further cooking. For the best flavor, 15 to 20 minutes of cooking is enough for most dishes.

Roasted chiles freeze well when prepared in the following way. Roast the chiles as directed above, preferably on a grill. As each chile is done, transfer it with tongs to a baking rack over a baking pan. When all the chiles have cooled to room temperature, place them on metal jelly roll pans or cookie sheets and freeze until they are hard. Transfer to plastic freezer bags, label and date, and store in the freezer until needed. To use, thaw the chiles for about an hour. The skins slip off very easily, and the seed membranes are usually easy to cut as well. Flavor and texture are best the first six months, but with care in removing as much air as possible from the freezer bags, and with a reliable freezer, we have used year-old frozen chiles and found them quite acceptable—even a treat when good market or garden peppers are not yet available.

Small and medium-sized fresh chiles without tough skins—de árbol, cayenne, Fresno and Santa Fe Grande, habanero, jalapeño, ornamental, piquín and tepín, rocotillo, tabasco, and Thai—are most often sauteéd or stir-fried; they need only a little cooking, from 5 to 10 minutes. They may be cooked whole or stemmed and seeded (wearing rubber gloves), left in halves or cut into pieces as you wish. Small chiles also may be added, whole or in pieces, to soups, stews, and sauces.

DRIED AND GROUND CHILE

Dried chiles offer completely different flavor experiences from fresh ones. They taste earthier, with nutty, fruity, smoky, or chocolate-like flavor compo-nents, and have a chewy texture. Not all varieties are pungent, but for those that are, the heat is strong because the chiles were dried at maturity. Therefore, wear rubber gloves when working with them. Soak or cook large dried peppers for at least half an hour to bring out the best flavor and texture. Often, recipes call for toasting dried chiles before grinding them; about a minute in an ungreased skillet over low heat is enough to bring out their aroma and flavor. Small, thin-walled chiles are usually used untoasted and whole in stir-fry dishes.

Properly dried and stored chiles are shiny and flexible, rather leathery. If bulk or packaged chiles are covered with chile dust, it usually indicates that they are old and/or have insects. Chipotles, which are smoke-dried jalapeños, have been dried until they are brittle, so they are not shiny, and they

Clockwise from upper left: dried chile de árbol, chipotle, New Mexico red, habanero, and ancho.

SEPTEMBER AND OCTOBER, WHEN YOUR GARDEN OR FARMERS' MARKET HAS A FLAMING CHILE PALETTE OF SCARLET, VERMILION, CRIMSON, AND MAHOGANY, IS THE TIME TO DRY CHILES.

may be dusty. Ristra chiles will probably have been dried under the right conditions, but they may have been stored for a long time. To ensure freshness, order them from New Mexico after the harvest and curing in late October. (See Sources, page 93, for New Mexico companies that ship ristras.) Because ristras that are hung for decoration collect dust and attract insects, inspect the chiles before cooking with them, and rinse if necessary.

Some thick-fleshed chiles—New Mexico, California, poblano, and mulato —and thin-fleshed ones— Thai, cayenne, piquín, and tepín—are commonly dried. If you grow your own, you can dry most varieties, including ornamental peppers, which are all edible and very hot. Fleshy cherry, banana, Fresno, jalapeño, and Santa Fe Grande chiles are usually pickled.

September and October, when your garden or farmers' market has a flaming chile palette of scarlet, vermilion, crimson, and mahogany, is the time to dry chiles. Discard any peppers that have insect damage, black spots or mold, or soft spots. If the weather is rainy or very humid, it is important to check the chiles in your garden carefully and wait until a dry spell to harvest them. Pick large chiles individually while they are still firm and crisp; entire bushes of small peppers, except habaneros, can be pulled up and hung to dry.

The southwestern United States provides the best climate for drying chiles: hot, bright days, warm nights, and dry air. If the harvest season is like this where you live, you can spread your peppers on screens or tie them by their stems with twine or florists' wire into ristras. However, chiles can also be dried in less-than-ideal conditions. Where temperature and sunlight are uneven and humidity is high, leave chiles outside when the sun is bright, and bring them indoors at night and when it rains. Drying times vary greatly, but after a few to several days of partial sun-drying, you can finish drying the peppers in an oven. Depending on the size and moisture content of the chiles, drying will take from 1 to 24 hours in a 150°F (65°C) oven. A thoroughly dried chile will feel free of moisture yet flexible. Store oven-dried chiles in labeled, tightly closed glass jars.

Small varieties of peppers offer more options for drying. The whole plants can be hung upside down in a well-ventilated place, in the sun if there is sun, or in an attic, garage, or shed if it is rainy. Or pluck individual chiles from the plants and spread them on screens or flat baskets. Turn them once a day until they are complete-ly dry, yet not brittle. Or thread them through the stems with a needle and hang them to dry.

Dried chiles also come in the forms of chile molido, which is pure ground red chile; hot red pepper flakes, which usually contains some seeds; ground cayenne pepper; and hot and sweet paprika. These keep well for a year or so in tightly closed containers away from heat and light. Ground peppers packaged in cellophane or glass should be bright in color and free from foreign matter or insects. Some color variation from package to package is normal, according to variety of pepper and harvest. The best paprika comes from Hungary, and is marketed in this country in bright red-white-and-green tins.

Grinding a lot of chile is an operation most home kitchens are not equipped for, but half a cup (120 ml) or so of fiery small dried peppers can be easily ground into red pepper flakes in an electric spice grinder or a clean electric coffee mill. We don't recommend using your coffee mill for both coffee and chiles unless you like an eye-opening cup of java in the morning. Small amounts of large dried chiles can also be ground for individual recipes. To get a fine powder, toast large chiles lightly first and grind them in batches two or three times. Dried and ground chiles are rather expensive by weight; growing your own peppers allows you to have an abundance without paying the grocer.

CHILES IN THE GARDEN

SPACE AND SEEDLINGS

The first thing to consider when growing peppers is how much space you have in your garden to devote to them. They need an area 2 to 3 feet (60 to 90 cm) in diameter (depending on variety), full sunlight, and good soil. Chiles are good container plants if the containers are large enough. Small ornamentals can be grown in 5-gallon (19-liter) pots; jalapeños, serranos, and even poblanos have grown well for us in half whiskey and wine barrels, underplanted with small peppers or companion herbs and flowers. Select the kinds of chiles you like to eat—really hot, medium-hot, or mild, and the plants that appeal to you for the way they look in the garden—compact and brilliant ornamental peppers, big glossy-leaved bushes and fruit like New Mexicos and Anaheims, or mid-sized hot cherry and banana peppers. Finally, decide whether to sow your own seed or buy a few plants from a reputable grower.

Propagation should be timed to set seedlings out at the earliest time the climate is stable and warm, preferably in early spring. Choosing the time to set out peppers is a bit of a balancing act, especially in the northern tier of the United States and in Canada, because peppers like relatively short days and evenly warm nights. Plenty of warmth and light are good for germination and early growth, but flower and fruit set are best in 8- to 12-hour days with a night temperature of between 60° and 70°F (16° and 21°C). On the other hand, for growers in the southern tier of states, if night temperatures are above 86°F (30°C), no fruit set will occur.

Most peppers germinate well if you follow the practices outlined below. Use a sterile, soilless medium consisting of one part perlite to one part sphagnum peat moss; in some garden shops these are available premixed. Moisten the mix and spread it in flats or single-cell planting trays. Sow the seeds in rows in flats, or two seeds per cell in planting trays. Cover the seeds lightly with about 1/8 inch (3 mm) of mix, and spray or mist with water to settle the mix. Cover the flats or trays with plastic wrap and place them in a warm room. Check in a few days to be sure they are still moist; seeds germinate in one to three weeks.

As soon as the seeds begin to germinate, remove the plastic wrap and place

Tabasco peppers at various stages of ripeness.

the flats under grow lights suspended 4 to 5 inches (10 to 13 cm) above the flats. Any fluorescent fixture with one warm and one cool white tube can be used. Provide the seedlings with 16 hours of light a day for two weeks, and feed once a week with a soluble fertilizer that is high in calcium nitrate. Misting is the best way to provide water; the seedlings should not dry out nor be overwatered.

When the seedlings have two sets of true leaves, transplant them to small individual cell trays, or thin to one plant per cell if you started them in cell trays. Place the seedlings in a warm greenhouse or a sunny window for at least two weeks. Fertilize once a week, and water as necessary; quick, sturdy root development should take place now. The seedlings may be held for up to six weeks. Check them for yellowing; they may need more frequent fertilizing in more dilute concentrations.

When the weather is warm (68°–72° F/20°–22°C) and stable, chile pepper seedlings need to be hardened off—gradually acclimatized to outdoor conditions—for about two weeks before being planted in their final garden place. Place the seedling containers in a lightly shaded and wind-protected spot for a few hours the first day. Each day following, increase the time outside and allow the plants to receive more sun, until they are out for 24 hours. Be sure the plants are well watered and protected from wind.

Cultivation and Maturation

After the peppers have been hardened off, they can be set in the garden or planted into large pots or tubs. If the weather turns cold or rainy, protect the plants at night with plastic jugs, bottles, or spun-bonded row covers. Remove the plastic every morning before the sun heats up; you can leave row covers on until the plants begin to bloom.

Peppers grow best in a loamy soil with plenty of humus. The plants benefit greatly when organic matter, such as compost or aged manure, is worked well into the soil. A little greensand or wood ashes, good sources of potash, can also be worked in if your soil is on the acid side. Whether peppers are grown in the garden or in containers, good drainage is essential. Two to 3 inches (5 to 8 cm) of water a week will provide enough moisture to keep plants vigorous.

In climates with a short growing season, a black plastic mulch not only retains the moisture peppers like, it warms the earth, absorbs heat, and keeps weeds down. Pepper roots will not grow when the soil temperature is below 55°F (13°C), and black plastic can warm the soil enough to give gardeners who would not be able to bring peppers to harvest the chance to do so. Paper, hay, or straw also help retain moisture and inhibit weeds, but they do not warm the soil as black plastic does, so wait to apply them until the soil is thoroughly warm.

Seed-savers should avoid cross-pollination by planting sweet and chile peppers in separate areas of the garden; a stuffed bell pepper as hot as a jalapeño may not please your children or favorite uncle. Plant the peppers in rows 2 to 3 feet (60 to 90 cm) apart, with 18 to 30 inches (46 to 75 cm) between plants, depending on the mature size of the variety. Set the plants so that the soil level is about 2 inches (5 cm) below the lowest set of leaves. After transplanting, water and feed with a soluble fertilizer high in calcium nitrate; follow the manufacturer's directions for diluting.

Even and regular watering is very important for steady growth, abundant bloom, and heavy yields. Regular fertilization is also important. Fertilizer high in calcium nitrate and ammonium sulfate should be applied to the plants in small amounts every two weeks for two months.

Though seed catalogs may list shorter periods, most hot peppers require about three months to abundant production. Plants will begin to bloom in 45 to 60 days, climate conditions being good, and the first fruit may appear soon after, especially for small chiles, but real harvests take another month. Some, notably the habanero, take even longer.

To stimulate continuous flowering and fruiting and to promote large yields, harvest the first green peppers as soon as they are fully developed. These are usually not as hot or large as end-of-season peppers. Cut the stems about 1/2 inch (1 cm) above the pepper caps; branches, especially when they are chile-laden, snap easily. A mature pepper is evenly colored and firm. Green-mature chile peppers are very good eating; Anaheims and other long green chiles are marketed at this stage. But even harvesting a few immature peppers from your garden is better than having a meager harvest at the end of the season.

In the right climate, with good cultivation practices and continuous harvest-

Habanero pepper plants bear abundantly in one author's Maryland garden.

Ornamental varieties can be both decorative and tasty.

ing, pepper production can last from one to three months after the first harvest. Chiles left on the plant will ripen from green to their final colors progressively, providing a show of particolored peppers and a range of colors on the same plant that is always pleasing to the eye. Whether the chiles ripen to orange, red, or mahogany, they then have the fullest flavor and the most pungency.

INSECTS AND DISEASES

Pepper plants can attract a number of varieties of pests, although usually only one or two kinds are a problem in any given area. Check with your local Cooperative Extension agent to see whether aphids, cutworms, flea beetles, leaf miners, maggots, or pepper weevils are likely to cause trouble for your plants. Though most of our pepper seasons have been relatively free of insect pests,

we have had the odd year of pepper weevil plague. To keep insect populations in check, inspect plants regularly, hand-pick or water-spray insects from plants (especially seedlings), inspect plants regularly, keep plants well-weeded, and use insecticide only if necessary. A relatively benign and effective pesticide is Safer's Insecticidal Soap.

Diseases that afflict chile peppers include anthracnose, leaf spot, and various mosaics. Mosaics present the biggest threat; they mottle and/or stunt leaves, and can kill plants. They are viruses spread by aphids, or in the case of tobacco mosaic, by tobacco. Smokers should not smoke near pepper plants, and should wash their hands before tending plants or harvesting peppers. Plants afflicted with mosaic should be removed and disposed of. Do not plant peppers near cantaloupes, cucumbers, or tomatoes, as they are also susceptible to tobacco mosaic. Soft spots on chiles are usually caused by the fungus disease anthracnose, which is spread by spores and most prevalent during wet weather. Leaf spot is seed borne, and is most common in sweet peppers. Plants with this disease lose leaves, exposing fruit to the sun and sunscald. Be sure your seeds are free of disease, or talk to your county agent about spraying.

Choices and Companions

More chile varieties than ever before are available to the home gardener. (See page 83 for seed companies that specialize in chiles.) Pepper plants and their fruits are quite decorative, in the garden as well as on the table. The large capsicums—Anaheims, New Mexico varieties, pasillas, poblanos, and mulatos—are produced on large plants that usually need staking, as well as space to grow without competition. Medium-sized chiles—

bananas, cayennes, cherry peppers, Fresnos, habaneros, jalapeños, rocotillos, Santa Fe Grandes, and serranos—grow on smaller bushes, but often need some support. Small hot chiles and ornamental peppers are grown for the dazzling colors they bring to the garden as much as for kitchen use. The plants are small but dramatic, adding bright color in borders or as accent plants. Tabascos are an exception: bushes can grow 4 to 5 feet (1.2 to 1.5 m) tall, and need staking. The chiles from ornamental plants, as well as piquíns, Thais, and tepíns, are small and very pungent. These peppers dry well and can make striking wreaths and arrangements.

Many people grow chiles according to the dishes they like to make with them. Large varieties can be eaten green—stuffed, in sauces and stews—or allowed to ripen red, then dried. In the green stage, their thin skins

are removed by roasting and peeling. Medium-sized chiles are eaten fresh in salsas and salads, cooked briefly in stir-fried dishes, sautés, or sauces, and pickled. Small chiles are occasionally eaten fresh in salsas, and commonly dried for decorative and kitchen use.

Herbs are excellent chile companions, both in the garden and the kitchen. They may be planted next to peppers, where they will add contrasting texture and color, and fragrance to attract bees for pollination. Basil, coriander, epazote, garlic, garlic chives, mint, marjoram and oregano, and sage are herbs that enhance the flavor of chiles. If you have room, it is nice to grow vegetables that go especially well with chile peppers. Cabbage, corn, eggplant, onions and scallions, pumpkins, summer squash, sweet peppers, tomatillos, and tomatoes all complement chiles and bring out their flavor.

Pepper Name	Other Names & Substitutes	Pungency	Pepper Size length/width		Plant Size height/space apart	
Ají	Ají amarillo, ají verde, habanero, long green chile	Very hot to fiery	4"–6"	¾"–1¼"	4'–6'	3'–4'
Anaheim/ New Mexico	California, chile verde, New Mexico, Big Jim, Chimayo, Hatch, Sandia	Mild to very hot	6"–7"	1"–1¾"	2'–3'	2½'–3'
Banana/ Hungarian	Hungarian wax, sweet, yellow wax, cubanella, gypsy, Roumanian	Mild to hot	4"–6"	¾"–1"	2'–3'	2½'–3'
Cascabel	Chile bola, bolita	Fairly hot to hot	¾"	1½"	1½'–2'	2'–2½'
Cayenne	Finger pepper, Ginnie pepper, jalapeño, japoné, Thai	Hot to fiery	3"–6"	¼"–¾"	1½'–2'	2'–2½'
Cherry	Creole cherry, hot or sweet cherry, red hot cherry	Medium to very hot	1½"–2½" diameter		1½'–2'	2'–2½'
De Árbol	Chile de árbol	Very hot	2½"–3½"	¼"	1½'–2	2'
Fresno/ Santa Fe Grande	Güero, güerito hot chile, caribe, caloro, diablo	Slightly hot to very hot	2"–4"	¾"–1½"	1½'–2'	2'–2½'
Habanero/ Scotch Bonnet	Bonnet, Bonnie, Scots, Congo, Guinea pepper	Fiery to incendiary	1"–1½" diameter		1½'–2½'	2½'
Jalapeño	Chipotle (when dried), chile gordo	Very hot to fiery	2"	½"	1½'–2'	2'–2½'
Japonés	Japanese peppers, hontaka, santaka, Thai	Hot to very hot	2"–3"	½"–1"	2'–3'	2½'–3'
Mirasol	Guajillo (when dried), cascabel long, mirasole, puya, pullia	Fairly hot to hot	2"–3"	½"–1"	1½'–2'	2'–2½'
Mulato	Poblano, ancho	Mild to fairly hot	3"–6"	2½"–4"	2'–2½'	2½'–3'

Colors ripening	Colors on maturity	Uses	Comments
Bright green-yellow	Golden yellow	Dries well; used as a condiment and in salsas and sauces.	Called cusqueño in Peru
Medium green to dark bright green	Red	Dried in ristras when red; greens are roasted and peeled or frozen and used in soups, stews, and rellenos	Referred to as chile colorado when red, and chile verde when green
Yellow-green, yellow, golden, orange	Bright orange-red to scarlet	Does not dry well; used fresh in salsas and sauces, good for pickling	Best eaten in the pale yellow-green and green stage
Dark green	Dark reddish-brown	Dries well; good in soups, stews, sauces, and sausage	Small, round pepper; slightly nutty in flavor when dried
Medium bright green	Bright red	Good dried and ground; can be used fresh; used in soups, stews, and sauces	Handsome dried for kitchen or decorative use
Medium dark green	Scarlet red	Does not dry well; good pickled whole or made into relish or jelly	Round and fleshy; lots of pulp for jelly making
Green	Red	Dries well; used in soups, stews, and beans	Used fresh in season, most often found dried
Lt. green, golden with rosy blush, orange red, red	Bright orange red to red	Most often fresh, pickled or used in salsa	This group of similar peppers has the most variations in flavor and size
Green to yellow green	Golden yellow-orange, scarlet to mahogany	Usually consumed fresh; good with lime; preserves well	Distinct fruit flavor, thrives as a perennial in the tropics and grows more than 6' tall, slow to bloom and set fruit
Bright dark green with purple or black tinge	Purple-black to bright deep red	Used fresh in salsas, sauces, beans, escabeche; dried for sauces and with beans	Smoke-dried chipotles can be found in adobo sauce, green peppers can be roasted; dries best by smoking
Bright green	Red	Used in sauces and stir-fried dishes; use like a cayenne	Dried red are ground for seasoning
Bright green to red	Brownish red	Used in stews and sauces; gives food a yellowish color when dried	Has a slightly fruity taste when dried; a favorite Mexican dried chile
Green to dark green with red-brown cast	Red-brown	Used fresh, but most often sold dried ground in a paste for moles, good with beans and in soups and stews	Dries to a deep chocolate brown-black; chocolate flavor

Pepper Name	Other Names & Substitutes	Pungency	Pepper Size length/width		Plant Size height/space apart	
Ornamental	Candlelight, Fiesta, Fips, Fireworks, Holiday Cheer, pequin	Hot to fiery	1″–2″	¼″–½″	12″–15″	1½′
Pasilla	Black chile, chile negro, pasilla negro, chilaca when fresh	Mild to fairly hot	5″–7″	¾″–1″	2′–2½′	2½′–3′
Pepperoncini	Sweet Italian pepper, golden Greek	Mild and sweet to slightly hot	2″–4″	½″–¾″	1½′–2½′	2′–2½′
Piquín/ Tepín	Pequín, chile pequeño, chiltecpin, chiltepequín, petine, bird pepper	Very hot to fiery	½″	¼″	12″–15″	1½′
Peter	Penis pepper	Very hot to fiery	1″–2½″	½″–¾″	1½′–2½′	2′–2½′
Poblano/ Ancho	Ancho (when dried), mulato, pasilla	Mild to hot	3″–5″	2″–3″	2′–3′	2½′–3′
Rocotillo	Red squash pepper, mushroom pepper	Mild to fairly hot	1″–1½″ diameter		1½′–2½′	2½′
Serrano	Chile verde, serranito, típico	Very hot to fiery	1″–2″	½″	2′–3′	2½′–3′
Tabasco	Louisiana, cajun	Very hot to fiery	1″–1½″	¼″	2′–3′	2½′–3′
Thai	Ornamental pepper	Very hot to fiery	½″–1″	¼″	12″–15″	1½′

Colors ripening	Colors on maturity	Uses	Comments
Cream, pale green, yellow, orange, and purple	Scarlet to deep red	Dries well and can be used in stir-fries, soups, and stews; used most often for decoration	Shapes vary; round, conical, elongated; some varieties have little flavor
Dark green with purple brown tinge	Chocolate brown	Can be used fresh in sauces, soups, and stews, good dried in chile powders, molés, soups, and sauces	Dries to dark raisin brown; lends an earthy, slightly bitter richness to foods
Green	Red	Can be dried; most often used green or pickled	Found bottled at the grocery as Italian pickled peppers
Medium green/ bright medium green to red	Scarlet/bright red brown	Can be used fresh, dried, or frozen; good in soups, stews, and beans; good hot dried pepper flakes	Dries to bright red-brown; sometimes used in commercial vinegared hot sauces
Light bright green	Golden yellow or red	Not much flavor; used more often as an ornamental	Conversational pepper due to shape and name
Dark green with purple-black cast	Deep red-brown	Dries well; used in molés and chili powder; when fresh it is best roasted and peeled and made into sauce or rellenos	The true chile relleno pepper; dried it becomes slightly sweet and fruity
Green to yellow green	Deep red	Does not dry well; used fresh in condiments, salsas, and sautééd as a vegetable	Looks like a small, pattypan squash
Medium dark green	Scarlet red	Dries well; good fresh or dried with beans, in soups, sauces, and stews; good red or green used fresh in salsas	Can be roasted; good dried for decorative use
Bright green	Bright orange-red	Dries well, though is generally made into fermented pepper sauce or packed in vinegar; not often used fresh	Used commercially to make Tabasco pepper sauce; plant grows over 5' tall in the South; heat lingers.
Bright medium green to red	Glossy deep red	Dries well; used fresh or dried in soups, sauces, stews, and stir-fries	Most often used in Thai and Oriental cooking; a good small, decorative dried chile; heat lingers

APPETIZERS AND FIRST COURSES

Yucatán-Style Ceviche

YUCATÁN-STYLE CEVICHE

Serves 6

Yucatecos esteem the habanero, the hottest, most perfumed, and most expensive of all chile peppers, and have developed an extensive repertoire of dishes around it. If you can't find habaneros, use six or eight jalapeños. For ceviche, absolutely fresh fish and shellfish are necessary; the enzymatic action of the lime juice on the seafood protein will "cook" the flesh but will not disguise any old or off-flavors. Fresh shrimp are hard to come by in many American markets; be sure that "previously frozen" ones have been flash-frozen at sea and not thawed until the day you purchase them. The dish will keep for a day or two in the refrigerator but is most flavorful on the day it is made.

1½ pounds (675 g) firm white fish fillets such as halibut, cod, or sea bass
3/4 pound (340 g) large (16–24 count) shrimp
1 large sweet onion such as Vidalia, Maui, or Walla Walla
3 or 4 habaneros, toasted lightly on an ungreased skillet for about 5 minutes
1 cup (240 ml) fresh lime juice
1/2 cup (120 ml) fresh orange juice
Salt

Cut the fish in 1/4-inch (5-mm) slices; remove any bones as you go. Place the fish in a glass or glazed ceramic dish large enough to hold it in one layer.

Shell and devein the shrimp, rinsing them only if necessary to rid them of grit. Slice the shrimp in half lengthwise or butterfly them. Layer the shrimp over the fish.

Slice the onion in half lengthwise, then crosswise in thin slices. Layer the onion over the fish and shrimp.

Wearing rubber gloves, stem, seed, and sliver the habaneros and scatter them over the onions. Season the dish with salt and pour on the lime and orange juices. Cover and marinate in the refrigerator for 8 hours or overnight, or until the fish and shrimp are opaque. Serve at cool room temperature.

CRAB AND CORN SOUP WITH CHILES

Serves 6

1½ quarts (1½ liters) chicken broth

3 slices fresh ginger about 7/8 inch (2 cm) across, peeled

1 4-inch (10-cm) piece fresh lemongrass, quartered lengthwise, or substitute 1 teaspoon (5 ml) each lime juice and grated lime zest

2 tablespoons (30 ml) Thai or Vietnamese fish sauce

2 garlic cloves, chopped coarse

3 or 4 small fresh hot chiles such as Thai, japonés, or serrano

3 or 4 green onions, trimmed with about 3 inches (8 cm) of green

Kernels from 3 ears fresh corn

1/2 cup (120 ml) unsweetened coconut milk

1 pound (450 g) lump crab meat, cartilage removed

Place the broth, ginger, lemongrass, fish sauce, and garlic in a noncorrodible pot. Bring to a simmer and cook for about 15 minutes.

Meanwhile, wearing rubber gloves, remove the stems from the chiles and slice the chiles thin on a diagonal. Slice the green onions thin on a diagonal.

Taste the broth and adjust the seasoning with a little more fish sauce if necessary. Oriental cooks usually leave the aromatics in the soup, but you may strain the broth before serving if you like.

Add the chiles, green onions, corn, coconut milk, and crab meat, and barely simmer about 5 minutes, or until the corn is cooked. Serve hot.

If you can find live crabs to steam, the crab flavor in this soup will be more pronounced than if you use frozen crab. Steam 2 pounds (900 g) of crab over plain water for about 12 minutes, then cool the crab to room temperature. Remove the meat, roe, and crab "butter", if any. Chop the shells with a cleaver. Barely cover them with water and simmer for about 15 minutes. Strain the broth and use it to replace some of the chicken broth in the recipe. Add the roe and butter when you add the crab meat. The soup is excellent before or after any flavorful Oriental main course, especially those with fish or chicken.

Fajita Taquitos

According to legend, history, and The Official Fajita Cookbook, *skirt steak—the tough muscle from beef diaphragm—was given to the ranch hands and cowboys who worked in Texas. These unnamed workers, often Mexicans, devised a way to make this "throwaway" meat tasty and tender, and called it* fajita, *Spanish for "cummerbund" or "little belt". Now that fajitas have become popular, most butchers charge a fancy price for this cut. We usually make fajitas of round steak, which is less expensive but just as delicious. Mesquite charcoal or dry mesquite wood will give an authentic Texas touch.*

2½ pounds (1.1 kg) round or skirt steak
4 or 5 garlic cloves, peeled and crushed
1 tablespoon (15 ml) dried Mexican oregano, crumbled
1 tablespoon (15 ml) toasted and ground cumin
2 teaspoons (10 ml) whole dried piquín, chiltepín, bird, or other very small hot peppers
2 limes
Salt
2 dozen 5- to 6-inch (13- to 15-cm) corn tortillas
Salsas, page 73–78
Guacamole, page 44

If you are using round steak, trim the meat of extra fat. Score the meat with a sharp knife along the grain, taking care not to cut more than about 1/8 inch (3 mm) deep. Score in the opposite direction to make crosshatching. Turn the meat and score on the other side.

If you are using skirt steak, trim the steak of membrane, or ask the butcher to do this. Trim the meat of extra fat and score it about 1/16 inch (1.5 mm) deep, as above.

Crush the garlic and mix it with the crumbled oregano, the cumin, and the hot peppers. Wearing rubber gloves, rub the mixture all over the meat. Marinate the meat, covered, in the refrigerator for 24 hours, turning once or twice.

Prepare a medium-hot wood or wood charcoal fire. Squeeze a lime over one side of the meat, rubbing the juice in well. Turn the meat and repeat with the remaining lime.

Grill the meat about 3 minutes on a side for round steak and about 2 minutes on a side for skirt steak, or until it is pink and juicy inside. Salt it lightly and let it rest for 5 minutes or so before cutting it into strips on a diagonal across the grain. Place three or four strips on two tortillas and serve.

Fajitas are simple, primitive, and messy finger food. They are best cooked and eaten outdoors with a variety of salsas, guacamole, beer, and plenty of paper napkins or towels.

GARDEN-STYLE GUACAMOLE TOSTADAS

These tostadas are lively with color, flavor, and texture. The guacamole vegetables are cut into bite-sized pieces, which are more appealing to eat than the usual mashed or pureed version. This is an easy recipe to double or triple for a crowd. You can prepare all of the ingredients in advance and assemble them at the last minute. Cover the guacamole tightly with plastic wrap; leaving the avocado pits in the mixture until time to serve seems to help prevent the avocado flesh from darkening. Heat store-bought tostada shells briefly before using, or quickly fry corn tortillas to crisp them; drain them well. Serve with salsas, chopped jalapeños or serranos, and sour cream if desired.

2 avocados, peeled, quartered lengthwise, and cut crosswise into 1/8-inch (3-mm) slices

1 tablespoon (15 ml) lime juice, or to taste

1 medium tomato, cut into eighths lengthwise, then crosswise into 1/4-inch (5-mm) slices

1 bunch green onions (about 8), sliced thin

1 bunch radishes, topped, tailed, halved lengthwise, and sliced thin

1 large garlic clove, minced

2 or 3 jalapeños or serranos, stemmed, seeded, halved lengthwise, and thinly sliced

Salt and freshly ground pepper

3 cups (700 ml) shredded red or green leaf lettuce

About 1/4 cup (60 ml) chopped cilantro leaves

12 5-to 6-inch (13- to 15-cm) flat tostada shells

2 generous cups (500 ml) grated sharp cheddar cheese

Combine the avocado and lime juice in a mixing bowl and toss well. Add the tomato, onions, radishes, garlic, and chiles and toss gently. Season with salt and pepper and put the pits in the guacamole until ready to serve. In another bowl, toss the lettuce with the cilantro.

When ready to assemble, heat the tostada shells to crisp them. Place them on a serving tray or baking sheet. Divide the cheese evenly among the shells, spreading it out to the edges. Divide the guacamole evenly among the tostadas, spreading it not quite to the edges so that some of the cheese shows.

Garnish the tops of the tostadas with a handful of the lettuce mixture in the center of each so that some of the guacamole shows. Serve immediately.

FRESH TUNA AND SERRANO SALAD

1 to 1¼ pounds (about 500 g)
    fresh tuna, preferably from the tail
1 medium sweet onion
3 tablespoons (45 ml) olive oil
2 tablespoons (30 ml) sherry vinegar
Salt

4 to 6 serrano peppers, depending on
    hotness
Several sprigs fresh acilantro
1 quart (1 liter) mixed loose-leaf
    lettuces, cleaned

In this light first-course salad, the usually less-expensive tail portion of the tuna is used to good result. We like to serve this salad while the main course is on the grill: vegetables, lamb, hamburgers, chicken, or fish. Try garnishing it with a diced ripe tomato or halved cherry tomatoes, or serving the salad on a bed of grated zucchini that has been blanched for 30 seconds, squeezed dry, and tossed with a little vinegar, oil, and salt and pepper. Jalapeños may be used instead of serranos; if they are hot, you will need fewer of them.

Cut the tuna and the onion in about 1/3-inch (8-mm) dice. Sauté them together in the oil over medium-high heat about 2 minutes, or until the tuna is just cooked through but still juicy. The onion will be crisp-tender. Toss the vinegar with the tuna and onion and season with salt.

Remove the tuna and onion to a bowl. Wearing rubber gloves, stem and seed the serranos and cut them in very small dice. Chop the coriander. Toss the tuna with the serranos and coriander. Refrigerate the salad, covered, for at least an hour.

Adjust the seasoning and serve the salad on a bed of lettuce at cool room temperature.

PEPPER AND CORN PANCAKES

Makes about 36 2-inch (5-cm)
or about 18 4-inch (10-cm)

*Pancakes are good for any
meal: breakfast, lunch, or
dinner. Two-inch (5 cm)
pancakes are just right for
appetizers, and 3 to 4
inches (8 to 10 cm) is a
good size for a side dish or
for breakfast. Use both red
and green peppers for
color. These are tasty
served as is, but we like
them with a little dollop of
sour cream and some
Green Chile Jelly,
page 81.*

1 cup (240 ml) stone-ground
    cornmeal
1/3 cup (80 ml) unbleached white
    flour
1 teaspoon (5 ml) baking powder
1/2 teaspoon (2.5 ml) baking soda
1/2 teaspoon (2 ml) salt
2 extra-large eggs
1 cup (240 ml) milk
1 tablespoon (15 ml) corn oil

2 or 3 jalapeño, serrano, or red hot
    cherry peppers, stemmed, seeded,
    and minced
1 garlic clove, minced
4 green onions, sliced thin, about
    1/2 cup (120 ml)
1½ cups (360 ml) fresh or frozen
    corn kernels
1 cup (240 ml) grated cheddar cheese

In a mixing bowl, combine the cornmeal, flour, baking powder, soda, and salt.

In a small bowl, beat the eggs lightly and add the milk and oil. Pour the liquid ingredients into the cornmeal mixture and add the vegetables and cheese. Blend well but do not overmix.

Heat a lightly oiled griddle or skillet over medium heat. Use about 1 tablespoon (15 ml) of batter for 2-inch (5-cm) pancakes and about 2 tablespoons (30 ml) of batter for 4-inch (10-cm) pancakes. Drop the batter onto the griddle and cook the smaller pancakes about 3 minutes on each side and the larger ones about 5 minutes on each side. They should be golden brown. Keep the pancakes warm in a medium oven while cooking the remainder. Serve hot.

SAUCES

Red Chile Sauce and Green Chile Sauce

Red Chile Sauce

This is a New Mexico-style chile colorado: pure chile flavor, simple to make, and very versatile. The recipe is easily doubled. The sauce keeps, tightly covered, in the refrigerator for about 2 weeks and in the freezer, packed to fill the containers completely, about 3 months. We usually buy pure ground red chile from New Mexico, where it is often called chile molido (see Sources, page 94). The sauce will be as hot as the chile molido used. Some New Mexican molidos labeled "medium-hot" are quite hot. You may prefer to buy both "mild" and "medium-hot" molidos and mix them.

1 medium onion, diced fine
3 garlic cloves, minced
2 tablespoons (30 ml) cooking oil
1 cup (240 ml) ground red chile, preferably New Mexican
1 teaspoon (5 ml) toasted and ground cumin

1 tablespoon (15 ml) fresh Mexican oregano, or 1 teaspoon (5 ml) dried Mexican oregano, crumbled
6 cups (1.5 liters) cold water
Salt

In a heavy covered pot, soften the onion and garlic in the oil over low heat for about 20 minutes. Add a few drops of water if necessary to keep the vegetables from browning.

Add the ground red chile, cumin, and Mexican oregano and stir the water in gradually. Simmer 30 to 40 minutes over medium heat, or until the sauce is medium thin. Season lightly with salt.

This sauce is commonly used as an enchilada or taco sauce, or with a little vinegar as a marinating and braising sauce for pork, chicken, and rabbit. If you cook over a low fire, it can be used as a marinade for grilled meats. Thin it with sour cream, broth, or tomato sauce to use as a mild enchilada or taco sauce, or a table salsa. It is good to top fried eggs for quick huevos rancheros. A spoonful or two will give a nice New Mexican touch to vegetable soups such as corn chowder, potato or tomato soup, or minestrone.

Roasted Chile and Herb Sauce

2 large poblano chiles
2 large Anaheim or New Mexico
  chiles
1 cup (240 ml) packed cilantro
  leaves
2/3 cup (160 ml) packed basil
  leaves
1/3 cup (80 ml) packed Italian
  parsley leaves

1/3 cup (80 ml) hulled pumpkin
  seeds, lightly toasted
4 large garlic cloves
3/4 cup (180 ml) freshly grated
  pecorino romano cheese
About 1/3 cup (80 ml) extra-
  virgin olive oil
About 1/4 cup (60 ml) water

This sauce is similar to both Mexican pipián verde and Italian pesto, with a Southwestern touch. It is delicious on pasta, potatoes, squash, and sliced fresh tomatoes or with grilled chicken and fish.

Roast the poblano and Anaheim chiles, and peel and seed them wearing rubber gloves. In a food processor, combine the cilantro, basil, parsley, pumpkin seeds, garlic, chiles, and cheese.

Start the processor and pour in the oil in a steady stream. Add the water to thin the sauce. Taste for seasoning and add a little more cheese or olive oil to obtain the right balance of flavor. Toss with hot pasta, or garnish cooked vegetables or meat, and serve immediately.

Green Chile Sauce

Most green chiles in the United States are grown in the Rio Grande valley in southern New Mexico. Hatch and Las Cruces host chile festivals complete with recipe contests, queens and kings, as well as fairs, fiestas, and conferences. This green chile sauce is quintessential New Mexico style: simple so that the chile flavor can be appreciated. If you have only Anaheims or other mild New Mexico cultivars such as Numex Big Jim or New Mexico 6, add several roasted and peeled jalapeños for the necessary heat.

2 pounds (900 g) fleshy, hot green chiles, such as Sandia, Chimayo, or Mexico Improved
1 large onion, diced
5 or 6 garlic cloves, chopped
2 tablespoons (30 ml) cooking oil
5 or 6 sprigs fresh Mexican oregano or sage, or 1 ½ teaspoons (8 ml)
dried Mexican oregano or sage, crumbled
1 teaspoon (5 ml) toasted and ground cumin
2 cups (475 ml) water or broth
Salt

Roast the chiles. Wearing rubber gloves, peel, stem, and seed them. Do not rinse; a few charred bits add to the flavor of the sauce. Dice the chiles.

In a heavy covered pot over low heat, soften the onion and garlic in the oil.

Add the diced chiles, Mexican oregano or sage, cumin, and the water or broth. Season lightly with salt.

Simmer the sauce over low heat for about 15 minutes, or until it is quite thick but not dry; add a little water if needed. Adjust the seasoning. The sauce may be used as is or pureed if you like.

We like to use our home-grown poblanos for a deep green, earthy-flavored, and pungent sauce. If your sauce is too hot, you may decrease the heat with sour cream; we often mix equal amounts of green chile sauce and sour cream together and heat the sauce very gently without simmering. Green chile sauce may be served with enchiladas and burritos; mixed with meat, chicken, or beans for tacos and tostadas; used as the base of chile verde stew with pork, lamb, chicken, or beef; added to omelets or scrambled eggs, or poured on fried or poached eggs; and mixed with corn, zucchini, and potatoes (see Potatoes Baked with Onions, Green Chile, and Tomatoes, page 71). The recipe may be doubled; the sauce keeps, tightly covered, in the refrigerator for 2 or 3 days and in the freezer for about a month.

WALNUT, CAYENNE, AND CORIANDER SAUCE

Makes about 2 cups (500 ml)

Experts disagree whether this sauce comes from the Circassian region in Russia or the Turkish-Armenian border. We first came across it in a Russian restaurant in San Francisco, and were immediately impressed by how delicious it was. Since then we have found it a very useful sauce not only for poached chicken, which is what it most frequently accompanies in Russian and Near Eastern cuisine, but also for vegetables, particularly potatoes, green beans, beets, eggplant, cauliflower, and cabbage. Some cooks make the sauce with light cream rather than chicken broth and add a handful of fresh bread crumbs.

2/3 cup (160 ml) shelled walnuts, chopped coarse
3 or 4 garlic cloves, sliced thin
8 or 10 fresh cilantro sprigs, chopped coarse
1 large fresh red cayenne pepper, stemmed, seeded, and sliced thin, or about 1/2 teaspoon (2 ml) ground cayenne
1 1/2 cups (360 ml) chicken broth
Salt

Pound the walnuts, garlic, coriander, and fresh cayenne together in a mortar and pestle. If you don't have a mortar and pestle, grind the walnuts to a fine meal in a food processor or blender. Mince the garlic, coriander, and fresh cayenne together, then mash the mixture with the flat of a large chef's knife or cleaver.

If you are using ground cayenne, stir it and the herbs into the ground nuts. Place the mixture in a saucepan and stir in the chicken broth. Season lightly with salt. Simmer over low heat for about 10 minutes, or until the sauce is medium thick. Adjust the seasoning and serve hot.

MAIN COURSES

Caribbean-Style Pork with Hot Frying Peppers

CARIBBEAN-STYLE PORK WITH HOT FRYING PEPPERS

Any pale yellow-green mildly hot pepper can be used in this dish: Cubanelle, hot banana, Roumanian, or Santa Fe Grande. Pork tenderloins cook quickly and are lighter than the pork roast or chops used traditionally. For a Caribbean-style feast, serve the pork with black beans and/or rice, corn on the cob, and lime- or vinegar-dressed coleslaw or sliced tomatoes.

2 pounds (900 g) pork tenderloins
3/4 cup (180 ml) white vinegar
1/3 cup (80 ml) mild-flavored honey
4 or 5 garlic cloves
Salt and freshly ground black pepper
3 tablespoons (45 ml) olive oil

1 pound (450 g) yellow-green mildly hot peppers, stemmed, seeded, and sliced about 1/2 inch (1 cm) thick
1 large sweet onion, halved lengthwise, each half cut into 8 lengthwise pieces and separated into segments

Trim the thin layer of connective tissue and excess fat from the pork. Mix the vinegar and honey together in a dish large enough to hold the pork. Mash the garlic very well or put it through a press and add it to the dish. Marinate the pork, covered, in the refrigerator for 24 hours, turning two or three times.

Remove the pork from the refrigerator about an hour before ready to serve. Transfer to a plate and reserve the marinade. Preheat the oven to 400°F (200°C) for about 10 minutes. Meanwhile, heat 1 tablespoon (15 ml) of olive oil over high heat in an ovenproof sauté pan large enough to hold the pork without crowding. Salt and pepper the pork, and sauté it for about 7 minutes, or until it is well browned all over.

Baste the pork well with the marinade and transfer it to the oven. Roast the pork for about 10 minutes, or until the internal temperature reaches 160°F (71°C), basting two or three times with the marinade. When the pork is done, place it on a board. Let it stand while you cook the peppers and make the sauce.

In a large sauté pan over high heat, sauté the peppers and the onion in the remaining olive oil about 5 minutes, or until they are browned and crisp-tender. Season lightly with salt and pepper.

While the peppers are cooking, pour the remaining marinade into the roasting pan along with a little water and salt and pepper. Reduce the sauce by about half and adjust the seasoning. Slice the pork about 1/4 inch (5 mm) thick. Place the peppers on a serving dish, arrange the pork slices on top, and pour the cooking juices over all. Serve hot.

JERK CHICKEN

Originally, jerk was a marinade for wild and domesticated goat; over the centuries, it has come to be used with pork, chicken, and even fish. The bare essentials of the Jamaican national dish are allspice, Scotch bonnet peppers, thyme, and some kind of meat, all cooked over a slow fire. Scotch bonnet is a close relative of the habanero pepper and is used in many Caribbean dishes. If you can't find Scotch bonnets or habaneros, substitute six or eight hot jalapeños. Slow cooking keeps the meat moist and allows the marinade to permeate it. The amount of jerk in this recipe will marinate 4 to 5 pounds (about 2 kg) of meat. You may substitute pork roast or halved game hens for the

1 4- to 5-pound (2-kg) chicken
1 small onion, diced fine
1 bunch green onions with some green, sliced thin
2 or 3 Scotch bonnet or habanero peppers, stemmed and seeded
1½ tablespoons (22 ml) allspice berries, lightly toasted and ground

1 teaspoon (5 ml) freshly grated nutmeg
1 teaspoon (5 ml) cinnamon
1 tablespoon (15 ml) fresh thyme leaves, or 1½ teaspoons (8 ml) dried thyme
1 teaspoon (5 ml) salt

Joint the chicken or have the butcher do this. Remove any excess fat, rinse the meat well, and pat dry. Place the chicken in a dish that will hold the pieces in one layer.

Place the onion and green onion in a food processor. If you make the jerk paste in a blender, spice grinder, or mortar and pestle, start with about one-third of the onions and green onions and blend or pound well before continuing.

Add the chiles, allspice, nutmeg, cinnamon, thyme, and salt. Process to a fine paste. If you use a blender, you will need to add about a tablespoon (15 ml) of water to ease the grinding. Using a spice grinder, finish grinding in batches, then blend the paste together in a bowl.

Wearing rubber gloves, rub the jerk paste all over the chicken pieces, including under the skin. Cover and refrigerate the chicken at least 4 or as long as 24 hours.

Remove the chicken from the refrigerator about an hour before cooking. Prepare a slow wood or wood-charcoal fire. We use prunings from our bay tree; fruitwood would also be good. Lacking these, soak some smoking chips—preferably from fruitwood but hickory will do—to give the jerk an authentic smoky flavor and to keep the fire slow. A grill with a cover is very helpful: you can regulate the fire without having to tend it constantly. Soak some smoking chips in water if you are using charcoal.

Place the chicken on the grill and watch it carefully for the first 10 or 15 minutes. Add the smoking chips if you are using them, and cover the grill. Turn the chicken frequently. The chicken will be done in about an hour, the meat cooked through but still moist. Let stand 5 or 10 minutes before serving.

chicken. Jerk dishes are traditionally served with baked or boiled yams or sweet potatoes and thin slices of sweet onion. We like them as well with corn on the cob and a salad of onion, plenty of parsley, and lime juice.

CHILI CON CARNE

*Even though this dish has
a Mexican name—
usually abbreviated to
chili—it is not Mexican
but the invention of
Mexican and Anglo
cowboys who worked the
enormous ranches of south
and central Texas after
the Mexican-American
war in the mid-nineteenth
century. They made the
dish of what they had:
chiles and beef.
The Texan-English name
of the dish is "bowl of
red", described in lively
detail by Frank X.
Tolbert in his book of that
name. Simple as this
version is, you don't have
to be from Texas to enjoy
it. The secret is to use
inexpensive muscle meat;
steaks and roasts do not
stand up to the long,
slow cooking.*

4 to 5 pounds (about 2 kg) lean beef
  stew meat
3 tablespoons (45 ml) cooking oil
1 medium head of garlic, peeled and
  chopped
2/3 cup (160 ml) Chili Powder,
  page 86

2 cups (475 ml) water
Salt
1/4 cup (60 ml) masa harina,
  optional

Cut the meat into bite-sized pieces, or if you prefer, have the butcher grind the meat in a coarse chili grind.

Heat a 6-quart (6-liter) or larger pot over high heat. Add 1 tablespoon (15 ml) of the oil and heat until it just smokes. Add about one-third of the beef and brown well all over. Transfer the beef to a platter. Finish browning the beef in two batches, adding 1 tablespoon (15 ml) of oil for each batch and allowing the pot to reheat. Add half of the chopped garlic to the last batch.

Return the browned beef to the pot and add the chili powder. Add the water, stir well and season lightly with salt. Cover the pot with the lid set askew, and bring the chili to a simmer. Cook over low heat for 1½ to 2 hours, stirring occasionally and adding a little water only if necessary to prevent the chili from sticking.

During the last 30 minutes of cooking, remove the cover and add the remaining garlic. Stir in the masa harina if you like a thick chili. Adjust the seasoning with salt and serve hot.

A cluster of chili fixings are traditional and very good: diced sweet onion, oyster crackers, grated mild cheddar cheese, sliced jalapeños, and crushed piquíns.

SEA BASS WITH VEGETABLES EN ESCABECHE

2 to 2½ pounds (about 1 kg) sea
   bass fillets
2 teaspoons (10 ml) toasted and
   ground cumin
1/4 teaspoon (1 ml) cayenne

Salt
4 tablespoons (60 ml) olive oil
About 1 cup (240 ml) all-purpose
   flour
Vegetables en Escabeche, page 80

Cut the sea bass into scallops about 1/2 inch (1 cm) thick and remove the large bones. Mix the cumin with the cayenne. Wearing rubber gloves, rub the fish all over with the mixture. Salt the fish lightly.

Heat the oil over medium-high heat in a pan large enough to hold the fish without crowding. Use two pans if necessary. Dredge the fish scallops in the flour and place them immediately in the pan. Sauté the fish about 3 minutes on each side, or until opaque throughout.

Transfer the fish to a serving platter and cover with about half of the pickled vegetables, spooning on some of the liquid. Serve the remaining vegetables on the side.

This dish is quite simple, and the flavor of the fish comes through clearly. Use any very fresh white fish fillets that you like: cod, Pacific or red snapper, grouper, rock cod. It is a quick and refreshing summer main course that goes with many Mediterranean and Southwestern accompaniments, such as couscous, herbed bulgur or rice, beans or chick peas, corn on the cob, or sautéed fresh corn, and lettuce or tomato salad.

WHITE BEAN CHILI

This is a mildly hot but flavorful chili, perfect for tailgate picnics, fall camping and fishing trips, or any occasion when you want to serve people who like chili "but not too hot". It is good with full-bodied beers and simple, robust red wines such as Zinfandel. Any white beans may be used, but imported cannellini beans hold their shape well and contribute a nice creaminess. Like other chilis, it is best made a day ahead.

2 pounds (900 g) chicken breasts, skinned and boned, with large tendons removed
1½ quarts (1½ liters) chicken broth
1 pound (450 g) dried white beans, soaked overnight in cold water
6 mild dried New Mexico or California chiles, stemmed and seeded
1 tablespoon (15 ml) olive oil
2 onions, diced fine
4 garlic cloves, minced
2 teaspoons (10 ml) toasted and ground cumin

2 teaspoons (10 ml) toasted and ground coriander
1½ teaspoons (8 ml) dried Mexican oregano
Large pinch ground cloves
Large pinch red pepper flakes
Salt
1 to 1½ cups (about 300 ml) grated mild cheese such as monterey jack, longhorn cheddar, or muenster
About 1/2 cup (120 ml) chopped cilantro

Poach the chicken breasts in simmering chicken broth 5 to 7 minutes, or until they are just firm and white. Remove the breasts to a plate to cool.

Drain and rinse the beans. Place them in a large pot. Add the chiles and the simmering chicken stock. Cook 45 minutes to an hour, or until the beans are just firm-tender. Remove the chiles to cool.

Place the olive oil in a skillet over medium-low heat. Add the onions and garlic, and cook, covered, until the onions have softened. Meanwhile, shred the cooked chiles and slice the poached chicken.

Add the chile pieces, cumin, coriander, oregano, cloves, and red pepper flakes to the onions and garlic. Stir well and cook, uncovered, for 2 or 3 minutes. Add the mixture to the beans and season well with salt.

Simmer for 15 minutes or so. When ready to serve, add the sliced chicken and just heat through. Serve hot in warm bowls, garnished with cheese and chopped cilantro.

Black Bean Chili

Even though this chili is meatless, it is nonetheless hearty, especially when served with its array of garnishes: we usually accompany it with warmed tortillas, corn bread, or corn chips. The chipotles—smoke-dried jalapeños—lend a rich, smoky flavor to the dish; if you don't have chipotles, substitute pasilla or ancho chiles. Adjust the amount of jalapeños or serranos according to how pungent they are and how hot you like it.

1 pound (450 g) black beans, rinsed, soaked, and drained

Water to cover

2 dried chipotle, ancho, or pasilla chiles, stemmed, seeded, and cut into large pieces

1 medium onion, diced

1 green bell pepper, stemmed, seeded, and diced

2 tablespoons (30 ml) corn or other vegetable oil

3 large garlic cloves, minced

2 or 3 jalapeños or serranos, stemmed, seeded, and diced

1 15-ounce (425-g) can tomatoes, diced

1 teaspoon (5 ml) toasted and ground cumin seed, or to taste

1 tablespoon (15 ml) fresh oregano, or 1 teaspoon (5 ml) dried oregano, crumbled

About 1 teaspoon (5 ml) salt

1/2 teaspoon (2 ml) Angostura bitters

1 to 2 tablespoons (15 to 30 ml) fresh cilantro, minced

Optional garnishes: sieved hard-boiled egg, grated sharp cheddar, sliced green onions, sliced jalapeños, sour cream

Barely cover the beans with water and add the dried chiles. Cook until the beans are barely done, adding more water if necessary. While the beans are cooking, sauté the onion and bell pepper in the oil over medium heat for 4 or 5 minutes. Add the garlic and fresh chiles and cook for another minute. Remove from heat.

Add the sautéed vegetables, tomatoes, cumin, oregano, and salt and stir well. Cook over medium-low heat for 15 to 20 minutes, stirring occasionally; add a little water if necessary.

Add the bitters and cilantro and cook 5 minutes longer. Taste for seasoning. Serve hot in bowls and pass the garnishes.

CHILE RELLENO ENCHILADAS

8 corn tortillas

8 large Anaheim, New Mexico, or
   poblano chiles, roasted, peeled, and
   seeded

About 2½ cups (600 ml) grated
   cheddar or monterey jack cheese or
   queso fresco

1 cup (240 ml) sour cream

1 cup (240 ml) fresh or prepared
   salsa

4 green onions, sliced thin with some
   green

We like chiles stuffed this way even better than classic chiles rellenos; the chile flavor stands out, and they are lighter because they aren't fried. Have all of the ingredients ready for assembling the enchiladas. Any sauce can be used, but this easy combination of sour cream and homemade salsa is simple and light.

Oil a 9-by-13-inch (23-by-33-cm) baking dish. Preheat the oven to 350°F (180°C).

Warm the tortillas on an ungreased hot griddle or *comal* so that they are pliable. Place a flattened chile across each tortilla and spread a generous handful of cheese along the chile. Roll the tortilla around the chile and cheese and place it in the baking dish. Repeat this process with the remaining tortillas.

Mix the sour cream and salsa in a small pan and heat until just warm.

Spoon the sauce evenly over the enchiladas and bake them for 15 to 20 minutes, or until hot and just starting to bubble. Serve hot, garnished with chopped green onions.

Eggs with Chiles and Tortillas

This is a quick, easy, tasty breakfast or brunch dish. Have all ingredients ready so that you can assemble the dish at the last minute. You may use jalapeño, serrano, red hot cherry, or güero peppers—one for a little heat or two for a hotter dish—or substitute Anaheim, New Mexico, or poblano chiles which you've roasted, peeled, stemmed, and seeded, then chopped coarse. The recipe is easily doubled.

5 extra-large eggs
2 teaspoons (10 ml) water
Salt and freshly ground pepper
2 tablespoons (30 ml) corn or vegetable oil
1/2 small onion, diced fine
1 garlic clove, minced
1 or 2 chiles, stemmed, seeded, and minced

3 corn tortillas cut into strips about 1/2 by 2 to 3 inches (1 by 5 to 8 cm)
2/3 cup (160 ml) grated monterey jack or sharp cheddar cheese
2 tablespoons (30 ml) chopped cilantro
Salsa, optional

Beat the eggs in a small bowl with the water, salt, and freshly ground pepper.

Heat the oil in a skillet, add the onion, and sauté over medium heat for about 3 minutes. Add the garlic and chiles, and stir and cook for 2 or 3 minutes longer. Add the tortillas, stirring until they absorb the oil and become pliable.

Stir in the eggs and when they begin to set, stir as if scrambling. Add the cheese and 1 tablespoon (15 ml) of the cilantro, and continue cooking the eggs to desired doneness. Garnish with the remaining cilantro. Serve hot and pass the salsa if desired.

VEGETABLES AND SALADS

Fruit Salad with Chiles and Lime

FRUIT SALAD WITH CHILES AND LIME

Serves 8 to 10

In Mexico, street vendors sell large pieces of watermelon, cantaloupe, and papaya sprinkled with ground red chile on sticks for easy handling. These are delicious, as are chile-sprinkled cucumber spears and roasted corn. The fruit juices, fresh chile, and lime in this salad create a surprisingly complex flavor: most people think it contains a liqueur. It is good, too, with half a teaspoon (2 ml) or so of ground red chile sprinkled over the fruit instead of the julienned fresh chile.

1/2 small watermelon
1/2 honeydew melon
1/2 cantaloupe
1 small pineapple

1 or 2 red serrano, jalapeño, or hot cherry peppers, sliced in very thin julienne
Zest of 1 lime
Juice of 1 lime

Seed the melons, cut the flesh into bite-sized pieces, and place them in a bowl. Cut the pineapple from its rind, remove the core, and cut the flesh into bite-sized pieces. Add the pineapple, chiles, and lime zest to the bowl and toss well. Drizzle the lime juice over the fruit and toss again.

Cover the bowl with plastic wrap and refrigerate for at least 1/2 hour. Taste and add a little lime juice if necessary. Serve cold.

CABBAGE CHILE SLAW

3 cups (710 ml) shredded green
  cabbage
3 cups (710 ml) shredded red
  cabbage
1 green or yellow bell pepper, julienned
1 red, orange, or purple bell pepper,
  julienned
1 large carrot, julienned, about 2 ½
  inches (6 cm) long
1 small red or yellow onion,
  quartered lengthwise and sliced
  thin lengthwise
3 jalapeño, serrano, red hot cherry, or
  Santa Fe peppers, stemmed, seeded,
  and julienned

2 garlic cloves, slivered lengthwise
About 1/3 cup (80 ml) olive oil
1/4 cup (60 ml) rice vinegar
1 tablespoon (15 ml) fresh oregano
  leaves, chopped, or 3/4 to 1
  teaspoon (4 to 5 ml) dried
  oregano, crumbled
1 ½ teaspoons (8 ml) toasted and
  ground cumin
1 teaspoon (5 ml) sugar
3/4 teaspoon (4 ml) salt, or to taste
Freshly ground pepper
Juice of 1/2 lime, or to taste

*Over the years, we've
become quite fond of
cabbage chile slaws, and
they are always popular
with our classes and
guests. This version is as
visually tantalizing as it
is tasty. We serve it as a
salad or relish, in soft
tacos, or on tostadas of
any kind. The more kinds
and colors of peppers you
use, the prettier and
tastier the slaw.*

In a large nonreactive bowl, combine the cabbages, peppers, carrot, onion, chiles, and garlic and toss well.

In a small bowl, combine the remaining ingredients except for the lime juice. Stir this vinaigrette well with a fork. Pour it over the vegetables and toss well to coat them.

Refrigerate the slaw for at least an hour. Toss with the lime juice. Taste for seasoning, adding a little more oil, salt, pepper, or lime juice if necessary. Serve the slaw at cool room temperature.

Spicy Noodle and Vegetable Salad

Serves 4 to 6

This is a versatile salad: add or delete whatever vegetables you like and use the noodles of your choice. Japanese soba or udon, Thai ba-mee egg noodles, Chinese wheat noodles, or linguine can all be used.

You may prepare the ingredients in advance and toss them together when ready to serve; the dressing is best drizzled on just before serving.

Noodles and Vegetables

1/2 pound (225 g) dried noodles or about 3/4 pound (340 g) fresh noodles, cooked al dente, rinsed under cold water, and drained well

2 teaspoons (10 ml) peanut oil

1 teaspoon (5 ml) toasted sesame oil

1 teaspoon (5 ml) soy sauce

1/4 pound (115 g) snow peas, topped, tailed, and cut diagonally

1/2 large red or purple bell pepper, cut into thin strips about 1½ inches (4 cm) long

1 carrot, sliced diagonally as thin as possible

Place the noodles in a bowl and toss them with the oils and soy sauce.

Place the snow peas in a colander, pour boiling water over them, and let them stand for 5 minutes. Run cold water over them and drain them well. Add the snow peas, pepper, and carrot to the noodles and toss well. Cover and refrigerate.

Dressing and Garnishes

2 tablespoons (30 ml) soy sauce

1 tablespoon (15 ml) and 1 teaspoon (5 ml) rice wine vinegar

1 tablespoon (15 ml) toasted sesame oil

3 tablespoons (45 ml) water

1 teaspoon (5 ml) sugar

2 garlic cloves

1 teaspoon (5 ml) freshly grated gingerroot

1 fresh red cayenne pepper or 2 or 3 Thai peppers, stemmed, seeded, and cut into pieces

About 10 Thai, spice, or lemon basil leaves, shredded

About 5 green onions, sliced thin with some green

1 generous cup (250 ml) mung bean sprouts, rinsed and drained

1 lime cut into 8 wedges

1/2 cup (120 ml) toasted peanuts, chopped

To make the vinaigrette, combine the soy sauce, vinegar, sesame oil, water, sugar, garlic, ginger, and chile(s) in a blender and blend until smooth.

To assemble the salad, drizzle the vinaigrette over the cold noodles and vegetables. Add the basil and half of the green onions and mung beans, and toss well.

Arrange the salad on a chilled serving platter and scatter the remaining green onions and mung beans over it. Squeeze two of the lime wedges over the salad and garnish the salad platter with the remaining wedges. Sprinkle the peanuts over the top and serve immediately.

PICO DE GALLO

In the southwestern United States, pico de gallo most often refers to a simple salsa of fresh tomato and hot pepper. In Mexico, it's a salad such as this one, made with oranges, jícama, and dried red peppers. It's good in late winter, when the oranges and jícama are at their peak and the bean and meat main courses need an accompaniment with lively flavor and texture. Growing your own thin-fleshed red chiles, such as cayenne, chiles de árbol, or Thai, will ensure that you have hot red pepper flakes. For instructions on drying chiles, see pages 26 and 27.

4 large navel oranges
2 pounds (900 g) jícama
About 1/2 bunch cilantro, chopped coarse
3 green onions, sliced thin with some green

Salt
1/4 teaspoon (1 ml) hot red pepper flakes, or to taste

Peel the oranges, removing the white inner skin. Cut them into slices or sections.

Peel the jícama and cut it into 1/4-in (5-mm) dice. Toss the jícama with the oranges. Toss in the cilantro and green onions. Season lightly with salt and add the hot pepper flakes. Let the salad stand for 30 minutes or so before serving.

POTATOES BAKED WITH ONIONS, GREEN CHILES, AND TOMATOES

1 ½ to 2 pounds (675 to 900 g) new red potatoes, scrubbed and cut into slices about 1/8 inch (3 mm) thick

Salt and freshly ground black pepper

2 medium onions, peeled, halved lengthwise, and cut crosswise into 1/8-inch (3-mm) slices

4 to 5 tablespoons (60 to 75 ml) extra-virgin olive oil

20 thyme sprigs about 2 ½ inches (6 cm) long, or 3/4 teaspoon (4 ml) dried leaves

12 fresh mint leaves, or 8 dried leaves

6 to 8 Anaheim or poblano chiles, roasted, peeled, seeded, and chopped coarse

3 large garlic cloves, cut in thin slivers

3 large tomatoes, cored, quartered lengthwise, and cut crosswise into 3/8-inch (8-mm) slices

This is one of our favorite casserole combinations; it is hearty and satisfying enough to serve as a main dish. We like to use small new potatoes, but larger potatoes work just as well if you halve them lengthwise before slicing them. The heat of this dish depends on how hot your chiles are: if you like it hot, use the larger amount of chiles. If you use dried herbs, crumble them as you scatter them over the layers of vegetables.

Oil a 9-by-13-inch (23-by-33-cm) baking dish. Preheat oven to 450°F (230°C).

Arrange half the potato slices in the dish. Season with salt and pepper. Scatter half the onion slices over the potatoes, and then half the thyme sprigs and mint leaves. Layer the remaining potatoes over the onions and herbs. Season with salt and pepper and sprinkle half the garlic over them. Drizzle with half the olive oil.

Layer the green chiles, then the remaining onion, thyme sprigs, mint, and garlic. Spread the tomato slices over the top and season with salt and pepper. Drizzle on the remaining olive oil.

Bake the casserole for 15 minutes. Reduce the heat to 350°F (180°C) and bake for 30 minutes longer. The top should be slightly charred, and the potatoes should be tender. Remove from the oven and cool for a few minutes before serving.

RICE AND ROASTED CORN AND PEPPER SALAD

It is worth the effort to fire the grill to make this salad—grilled corn and peppers and rice salads are among the great food pleasures of summer. We sometimes grill a chile pepper or two to add to the salad; and while the grill is hot, we grill some fish, chicken, or slices of eggplant and squash to serve with the salad. Other good accompaniments are grill-toasted thick slices of country bread rubbed with garlic, a plate of juicy red tomato slices, and ice-cold beer.

6 ears of corn in their husks
Olive oil for grilling
Salt and freshly ground pepper
2 sweet onions
1 red bell pepper
3 cups (710 ml) cooked rice
About 1/4 cup (60 ml) olive oil, or to taste

Juice of 1 lime, or to taste
1 tablespoon (15 ml) ground red chile, medium-hot or hot
3 garlic cloves, minced fine
1/4 teaspoon (1 ml) Angostura bitters
1/2 cup (120 ml) basil leaves, shredded

Pull the corn husks back and remove silk. Brush the kernels lightly with olive oil, season with salt and pepper, and pull the husks back around the ears. Peel the onions and cut them into slices about 1/2 inch (1 cm) thick. Brush them lightly with olive oil.

Place the corn, onions, and red pepper on a medium-hot grill. Cook the corn for 5 to 10 minutes, turning two or three times; cook the onions 4 or 5 minutes on each side. Roast the pepper 6 to 8 minutes, turning so the skin is blackened all over. Grilling time will vary according to the heat of the fire and the size of the vegetables.

Remove the vegetables from the grill. When they are cool enough to handle, cut the corn from the cob, chop the onion, and peel, stem, and seed the pepper. Cut the pepper lengthwise into strips and cut the strips into pieces about 1 inch (2 cm) long. Combine the vegetables in a bowl with the rice and toss well.

Combine the olive oil, lime juice, ground red chile, garlic, and bitters; season well with salt and pepper. Pour this dressing over the vegetables and rice. Add the basil, toss well, and taste for salt and pepper. Add more olive oil or lime juice if necessary. Let stand for at least 20 minutes before serving at cool room temperature.

SALSAS AND ACCOMPANIMENTS

Mango Salsa, Green Tomato Salsa, Chili Powder, Green Chile Jelly, and Pickled Peppers

Green Tomato Salsa

This is one of our favorite salsas for the end of summer, when a variety of ripe and unripe tomatoes are available. However, by keeping the proportions of tomatoes, onions, garlic, and hot peppers roughly the same, you can use all ripe tomatoes of any color, a sweet white or yellow onion, tomatillos instead of green tomatoes, Italian or Mexican oregano or even sage in addition to or in place of the cilantro.

A large part of salsa-making fun is in the individual touches. Whatever your touch is, make your salsa fresh and hot!

3 green tomatoes, about 1¼ pounds (560 g)

3 red, orange, pink, or yellow ripe tomatoes, about 1¼ pounds (560 g)

1 small red onion, diced fine

2 or 3 garlic cloves, minced

3 hot peppers, or to taste, stemmed, seeded, and diced very fine

1/4 cup (60 ml) chopped cilantro

1/2 teaspoon (2 ml) salt, or to taste

Core the tomatoes and remove most of the seeds. Cut in small dice and mix with the remaining ingredients. Let the salsa stand for an hour or so before serving.

HABANERO, TOMATILLO, AND ORANGE SALSA

Makes about 2 cups (500 ml)

1 pound (450 g) tomatillos
3 or 4 habaneros
2 oranges

1 bunch green onions, sliced fine with 3
   to 4 inches (8 to 10 cm) of green
Salt
Lime juice

In an ungreased skillet over medium heat, roast half of the tomatillos in their husks for about 10 minutes, turning frequently. Meanwhile, husk the remaining tomatillos, dice fine, and place them in a bowl. Cool the roasted tomatillos, then husk them and place them in a blender.

Roast the habaneros over low heat, turning occasionally, about 5 minutes, or until they are just soft and speckled with brown. Wearing rubber gloves, stem and seed the habaneros and add them to the tomatillos in the blender. Puree the mixture.

Squeeze one of the oranges and pour the juice into the bowl containing the diced tomatillos. Add the pureed peppers and tomatillos. Peel the other orange, removing the pith; seed if necessary and cut into small dice. Add the diced orange and the green onions to the salsa.

Season the salsa with salt and lime juice, and let stand for about half an hour before serving.

This is one of our favorite salsas and one that wins raves from habanero lovers in our cooking classes. It is simple and quick to make, and the recipe is easily doubled. It is tropical rather than Southwestern in flavor, but it can be used in any menu in which you want a hot salsa. It is rather addictive with white corn chips. Roasting tomatillos brings out their sweetness, and roasting the habaneros accents their fruity aroma and flavor.

MANGO SALSA

Fruit salsas have become the vogue in some parts of the country, with almost any kind of chile combined with almost any kind of fruit, including peaches and raspberries. To our palates, tropical fruits such as papaya, mango, and pineapple taste the best with chiles; melons also go well in fruit salsas. For Fruit Salad with Chiles and Lime, see page 66.

2 mangoes, cut in small dice
1 habanero or 3 or 4 hot chiles such as serrano or jalapeño, stemmed, seeded, and cut in small dice
3 or 4 green onions, sliced thin with some green

1 small red bell pepper, cut in small dice
1/4 cup (60 ml) chopped cilantro
Juice of 1 lime, or to taste
Salt to taste

Mix all the ingredients in a bowl and let stand for an hour to develop the flavor. Serve with poultry or fish, as a table salsa, or with tortilla chips.

RED CHILE SALSA

8 mild dried red chiles such as New
    Mexico or California
6 to 8 dried red chiles such as
    serranos, japonés, or chiles de árbol
3 garlic cloves, crushed

2 cups (475 ml) water
1/2 teaspoon (2 ml) salt, or to taste
2 teaspoons (10 ml) white vinegar,
    or to taste

This recipe is the result of a satisfying search for a salsa for winter, when flavorful fresh tomatoes and chiles are a distant dream. It has the bite and directness of a good restaurant salsa. It keeps, tightly covered, in the refrigerator for about 2 weeks.

Toast the chiles on an ungreased skillet or *comal* over low heat, turning them frequently, until they just give off an aroma. Cool; then, wearing rubber gloves, remove the stems and seeds.

Place the chiles in a blender with the garlic, water, salt, and vinegar; puree. Let the salsa stand for 30 minutes or so to develop the flavor. Serve with grilled meats, as a dipping salsa, with tacos, or as a base for tamale fillings or enchilada sauces.

PANTRY CHIPOTLE SALSA

This is a quick and easy salsa, particularly welcome in winter when good fresh chiles and tomatoes are hard to find. Though the price of chipotles—Mexican smoke-dried jalapeños—increased almost tenfold in the early 1990s, canned chipotles en adobo (a very hot and tangy tomato-and-vinegar sauce) are relatively reasonably priced. Most chipotle fans will eat them with anything, but we find that this salsa really picks up the flavor of plain broiled, grilled, or poached seafood and chicken. It is a fine table salsa with any Southwestern meal or snack.

3 or 4 chipotle chiles en adobo, or to taste
1 tablespoon (15 ml) adobo sauce
28-ounce (800-ml) can plain diced tomatoes

1 medium onion, diced fine
2 or 3 garlic cloves, minced
1 small bunch cilantro, chopped
Salt

Wearing rubber gloves, stem if necessary, dice the chipotles, and place them in a bowl. Add the remaining ingredients and season lightly with salt. Let the salsa stand for 30 minutes or so to develop the flavors.

CHIPOTLE, BEAN, AND SOUR CREAM DIP

About 2½ cups (600 ml) cooked or canned dried beans
1 to 1½ cups (240 to 360 ml) sour cream
1 or 2 chipotles en adobo, stemmed and chopped
1/2 small onion, quartered
2 garlic cloves, minced
Handful of cilantro leaves, optional
1/2 teaspoon (2 ml) toasted and ground cumin

Chipotles en adobo are a staple in most chile lovers' kitchens. The sauce that permeates and softens the smoke-dried chiles is a good seasoning for soups, stews, and beans. This dip makes use of leftover or canned beans; black beans are excellent, and pinto beans are also good. If you don't have canned chipotles en adobo, use two hot chiles of your choice. This is a good party dip for tortilla chips or slices of cucumber and jícama.

In a food processor, combine 1½ cups (360 ml) of the beans with 1/2 cup (120 ml) of the sour cream, the chiles, onion, garlic, and the cilantro if desired. Process until almost smooth, leaving a little texture.

Stir in the cumin and the remaining beans and sour cream. Taste for seasoning. You may need to add a little salt, more sour cream, another chipotle, or some adobo sauce.

Chill the dip for at least 30 minutes; it takes some time to develop the flavor. Remove from refrigerator 20 or 30 minutes before serving and serve at cool room temperature.

Vegetables en Escabeche

Vegetables en escabeche (a Mexican term for pickled that is commonly used in the Southwest) are wonderfully refreshing when the weather is hot and with hot food. Even though there are hot peppers in this recipe, the pickling liquid and the other vegetables combine with them to make the dish just piquant. The vegetables are good as an appetizer, relish, or accompaniment to sandwiches or soft tacos as well as simple fish dishes, such as Sea Bass with Vegetables en Escabeche, page 59. Make the recipe at least several hours ahead. It will keep, tightly covered, in the refrigerator for about a week.

3/4 cup (180 ml) white vinegar
2 cups (475 ml) water
1 teaspoon (5 ml) salt
1/2 teaspoon (2 ml) sugar
1 teaspoon (5 ml) dried Mexican oregano
2 cloves
1 3-inch (8-cm) cinnamon stick

1 medium red bell pepper
1 medium green bell pepper
2 or 3 jalapeños or other green hot chile peppers
2 or 3 red fresh serranos or other red hot chile peppers
1 medium carrot
1 large onion
3 garlic cloves

Bring the vinegar, water, salt, sugar, oregano, cloves, and cinnamon to a boil in a noncorrodible saucepan. Simmer the mixture while you prepare the vegetables.

Stem and seed the bell peppers. Cut them in half crosswise, then into thin slices. Wearing rubber gloves, stem and seed the chiles, then cut them into lengthwise slivers. Julienne the carrots. Peel the onion and cut it lengthwise into slivers. Peel and sliver the garlic.

Place the vegetables in a glass or stainless bowl and strain the pickling liquid over them. Cover the bowl and marinate in the refrigerator for at least 3 hours before serving, tossing occasionally. Serve at cool room temperature.

GREEN CHILE JELLY

1 generous pound (500 g) jalapeños
   or other hot green chile peppers
1 pound (450 g) green bell peppers
2 cups (475 ml) water
1 1/4 cups (300 ml) apple cider
   vinegar

1 1¾-ounce (50-g) package
   powdered pectin
5 cups (1200 ml) sugar

Savory corn pancakes garnished with this jelly and sour cream are reason enough to prepare a batch of this recipe. Bagels and cream cheese also make good use of this condiment, and our resident chilehead recommends a sandwich filling of peanut butter, sliced onion, and green chile jelly. We usually use jalapeños for this recipe, but serranos, or even a few poblanos or Anaheims, also work.

Wearing rubber gloves, stem and seed the peppers, and puree them as fine as possible in a food processor.

Combine the pepper puree and the water in a large noncorrodible pot and place over medium-high heat. When the liquid comes to a simmer, reduce the heat to medium and cook for about 10 minutes, stirring occasionally.

Pour the hot pepper puree into a jelly bag or a strainer lined with dampened cheesecloth. Let the juice drip for an hour, stirring occasionally.

Pour the strained juice into a noncorrodible pot; there should be 2 cups (475 ml). Add water to equal this amount if necessary. Add the vinegar and pectin and stir well.

Bring the liquid to a full boil and add the sugar all at once. Bring the contents of the pot to a boil that cannot be stirred down and stir for 1 minute.

Immediately ladle the hot liquid into hot sterilized jars, leaving 1/4 inch (5 mm) headspace, and seal. Refrigerate any jars that do not seal and use them within 2 weeks.

HOT AND SWEET PEPPER RELISH

Makes about 7 pints (3.5 liters)

The most ordinary backyard barbecue with grilled hamburgers and hot dogs becomes a little fiesta when this relish is offered. It makes any sandwich—tomato, cheese, tuna, or lunchmeat— zesty and is also good with an Indian menu. The recipe can be made hotter or milder by adjusting the proportion of hot and medium-hot chiles.

2 ½ pounds (1.1 kg) medium-hot and hot chiles of mixed colors
2 pounds (900 g) bell peppers of mixed colors
1 ½ pounds (675 g) green tomatoes
1 pound (450 g) red ripe tomatoes
1 ½ pounds (675 g) onions
8 to 10 garlic cloves
1 ½ cups (360 ml) vinegar
1/4 cup (60 ml) sugar
2 tablespoons (30 ml) pickling or kosher salt

Wearing rubber gloves, stem, seed, and dice the chiles or chop them in a food processor, using the pulse button. Place them in a large nonreactive bowl.

Stem, seed, and dice the bell peppers or chop them in a food processor. Add them to the chiles.

Core, seed, and dice the green and red tomatoes or chop them in a food processor. Add them to the bowl.

Dice the onions fine and mince the garlic. Add them to the bowl.

Stir in the vinegar, sugar, and salt. Transfer the mixture to a large nonreactive pan and bring to a boil. Reduce the heat to a vigorous simmer and cook 10 minutes.

Pack vegetables in hot sterilized canning jars and seal with hot scalded lids and rings. Process according to manufacturer's directions. Cool jars away from drafts. Store any jars that do not seal in the refrigerator, and use them within 2 weeks. Let the sealed jars stand for a week before using.

HOT CHILE OIL OR VINEGAR

1 ½ cups (360 ml) olive oil or distilled or white wine vinegar

1/2 cup (120 ml) dried hot peppers such as Thai, chiles de árbol, or cayenne, or 2/3 cup (160 ml) fresh hot peppers

These are handy condiments to have when you want to add just a touch of chile flavor to a dish—noodles, rice, fish, chicken, meat, vegetables, or salads. Any small hot chile will give good results; use dried peppers for oil and fresh chiles for vinegar. If the fresh peppers are large, such as jalapeños or habaneros, halve them lengthwise.

To prepare the oil, place the oil and dried chiles in a heavy noncorrodible saucepan. Heat them over low heat for about 10 minutes. Do not allow the oil to smoke or bubble. Remove from heat and cool to room temperature. Pour the contents of the pan into a jar with a tight-fitting lid and store in a cool, dark place. The oil will keep about 6 months; it will become hotter as it ages.

To prepare the vinegar, pierce whole, fresh chiles with a knife, and place the vinegar and chiles in a heavy noncorrodible saucepan. Heat over low heat for about 10 minutes. Do not allow the vinegar to boil. Cool to room temperature, then transfer to a jar with a tight-fitting lid. Or strain into a bottle, adding some pierced small fresh peppers if you like. The vinegar keeps a good chile flavor for about 6 months and then slowly loses its pungency.

PICKLED PEPPERS

Though jalapeños are the most common pickled peppers, we like pickled serranos, Hungarian hot, and red hot cherry peppers just as well, and they are pretty together. Use whichever chile peppers you have, all of one variety or mixed. Larger peppers can be cut in half, but don't use chiles that have tough skins such as New Mexico greens, Anaheims, and poblanos. We like to put up peppers in large quantities, but if this is too many peppers for you, just halve the recipe. Do not substitute table salt for pickling or kosher salt as it contains additives that cloud the liquid.

5 pounds (2.3 kg) jalapeños or other chiles

3 to 4 quarts (3 to 4 liters) cold water

2 cups (475 ml) pickling or kosher salt

10 cups (2400 ml) distilled white vinegar

2 cups (475 ml) water

2 teaspoons (10 ml) pickling or kosher salt

2 teaspoons (10 ml) each coriander, dill, and mustard seeds

1 teaspoon (5 ml) each cumin seed and black peppercorns

3 bay leaves

10 to 20 garlic cloves, peeled and halved if large

Wash the chiles and pierce the flesh of each one with a knife point.

Place the chiles in a large noncorrodible bowl, crock, or pot. Pour 3 to 4 quarts (3 to 4 liters) of water and 2 cups (475 ml) of salt over them and stir; weight them with a plate or lid so that the chiles are totally submerged. Let them stand at cool room temperature or refrigerate for 24 hours.

Drain the peppers, rinse them well in fresh water, and drain them again.

In a large noncorrodible pot, combine the vinegar, 2 cups (475 ml) of water, and 2 teaspoons (10 ml) of salt. Tie the pickling spices in cheesecloth or a muslin bag and add it to the pot. Bring the ingredients to a boil and simmer for 5 minutes.

Add the chile peppers to the pot and cook them for 3 minutes after the liquid has begun to boil.

Divide the garlic cloves equally among hot sterilized canning jars.

With a ladle or large spoon, pack the peppers tightly into the jars up to the bottom of the screw band. Ladle the hot pickling liquid into the jars, leaving 1/2 inch (1 cm) headspace.

Seal the jars with hot scalded lids and rings. Process the jars in a boiling water bath according to manufacturer's instructions.

Cool jars away from drafts. Refrigerate any jars that do not seal and use them within 2 weeks.

CHILI POWDER

In experimenting with making chili powders, our main motivation has been to have superior flavor and to avoid the excessive salt, monosodium glutamate, and other undesirable additives that sometimes are used in commercial chile powders. If you can't find all the dried chiles called for here, by all means experiment with what is available to you. Guajillos are a good addition for flavor, and japonés and piquíns are good for heat. The paprika here is for color and the cayenne, for heat; omit them if the powder suits you without them, or add more of each. Using many different dried chiles results in a chili powder that plays across your chili dishes and palate with a great deal of subtlety and resonance.

6 large California or New Mexico dried chiles
3 large dried ancho chiles
3 large dried mulato chiles
3 large dried pasilla or chile negro chiles
6 dried chipotle chiles
6 tablespoons (90 ml) cumin seed
6 tablespoons (90 ml) coriander seed
1 tablespoon (15 ml) whole cloves
6 tablespoons (90 ml) dried Mexican oregano
3 tablespoons (45 ml) paprika, optional
1 tablespoon (15 ml) ground cayenne, optional

Wearing rubber gloves, remove the stems and most of the seeds from the dried chiles. Break the chiles into large pieces. Over low heat, toast them in two or three batches on an ungreased griddle or skillet for about a minute. The chiles should just begin to smell fragrant. Do not let them darken or they will taste bitter. Cool the chiles to room temperature on a platter.

Over low heat, toast the cumin, coriander, and cloves on an ungreased griddle or skillet for about 3 minutes, or until they release their aroma. They should be lightly colored. Cool the spices to room temperature on a plate.

Break the chiles further by hand, wearing rubber gloves, or in a food processor. Grind them in small batches in a spice grinder or a clean coffee mill.

Grind the toasted spices and the oregano in small batches in a spice grinder or coffee mill. Mix the ground chiles and spices together. Grind again in small batches to make a fine powder.

Blend the paprika and cayenne well into the powder if you are using them. Store the chili powder in tightly sealed glass jars away from light and heat. Use within six months for best flavor.

DESSERTS

Chocolate Chile Pecan Brownies and Holy Moly Ice Cream

CHOCOLATE CHILE PECAN BROWNIES

Makes a 9-by-13-inch
(23-by-33-cm) pan of brownies

These rich chocolate brownies have a pleasant hot zing when you bite into a chile-covered pecan—the intensity of the chocolate teams well with the chile flavor and mellows the chile heat. If you have only a medium-hot ground red chile, add an extra teaspoon (5 ml) to the batter.

Caramelized Pecans

1/4 cup (60 ml) water
2 tablespoons (30 ml) sugar
1 cup (240 ml) coarse-chopped
   pecans

1 tablespoon (15 ml) hot ground
   red chile
1/4 teaspoon (1 ml) salt

In a small skillet, combine the water and the sugar and stir over medium heat for 2 minutes. Add the pecans and stir well with a wooden scraper as the water evaporates. After 3 or 4 minutes, add the ground chile and the salt and toss well to coat the pecans evenly. Continue stirring for a few minutes longer until all the water has evaporated, the pecans are coated, and the pan is dry. Turn the nuts onto a plate or waxed paper to cool.

Brownies

4 ounces (115 g) unsweetened
   chocolate
10 tablespoons (150 ml) unsalted
   butter
1½ cups (360 ml) sugar
   (castor sugar)
3 extra-large eggs

1¼ teaspoons (6 ml) pure vanilla
   extract (essence)
1 cup (240 ml) unbleached flour
2 teaspoons (10 ml) hot ground
   red chile
Generous pinch of salt

Preheat the oven to 350°F (180°C). Generously butter and lightly flour a 9-by-13-inch (23-by-33-cm) baking pan.

Melt the chocolate and the butter in a heavy-bottomed pan over low heat or in a heatproof bowl in the microwave. Stir well and let cool a few minutes. Beat the mixture with a wooden spoon until blended. Stir in the sugar and mix well.

Beat the eggs and the vanilla into the batter until well blended. Stir in the flour, ground chile, and salt until just mixed. Stir in the pecans and pour the batter into the prepared pan, spreading it evenly.

Bake for 25 to 30 minutes, or until a tester comes out clean. Cool in the pan on a rack, then cut brownies into pieces and remove them to a serving plate.

HOLY MOLY ICE CREAM

The chile flavor here is subtle, a warm, slightly lingering glow at the back of the palate and a rich spiciness. The ice cream is best on the day it is made, but we usually make the infusion the day before so that it can chill thoroughly overnight. Since the heat of chiles can vary, it is wise to taste the ones you will be using and use fewer if they are very hot. The method of softening dried chiles, then scraping the flesh loose from the tough skins, is one used by many Southwestern and Mexican cooks to make chile paste; it is time-consuming but worth the effort.

2 ounces (60 g) fleshy dried ancho chiles, about 3 large anchos
1/2 vanilla bean, split lengthwise
1 4-inch (10-cm) cinnamon stick
3 whole cloves
2 cups (475 ml) half-and-half (single cream)

1 cup (240 ml) whipping (double) cream
1 cup (240 ml) sugar (castor sugar)
5 ounces (140 g) bittersweet chocolate

Wearing rubber gloves, stem the chiles, cut them in half lengthwise, and remove most of the seeds.

Place the chiles, vanilla bean, cinnamon, and cloves in a heavy-bottomed saucepan. Add the creams and scald over low heat. Remove the pan from the heat and let the mixture steep for 1 to 2 hours, depending on how pliable the chiles are.

Scrape the flesh from the chile skins with the back of a knife. Place the chile flesh and about 2/3 cup (160 ml) of the scalded cream in a blender and puree. Return the puree to the scalded cream mixture.

Scrape the seeds from the vanilla bean into the scalded cream mixture. Strain the mixture through a sieve into a clean heavy-bottomed saucepan. Add the sugar and chocolate. Cook over low heat, stirring, until the sugar dissolves and the chocolate melts.

Transfer the mixture to a stainless steel bowl. Chill thoroughly in the refrigerator overnight or in an ice-water bath.

Pour the mixture into an ice cream freezer and freeze according to the manufacturer's instructions.

Sources

Fresh/Dried Chiles

Casados Farms, PO Box 1269, San Juan Pueblo, NM 87566

Chili Pepper Emporium, 328 San Felipe Road NW, Albuquerque, NM 87104

Coyote Cafe General Store, 132 West Water Street, Santa Fe, NM 87501

Josie's Best, 2600 Camino Entrada, PO Box 5525, Santa Fe, NM 87501

Los Chileros, PO Box 6215, Santa Fe, NM 87502

Mo Hotta Mo Betta, PO Box 4136, San Luis Obispo, CA 93493

Old Southwest Trading Company, PO Box 707, Albuquerque, NM 87194

Pecos Valley Spice Company, 800 Rio Grande Blvd. #14, Albuquerque, NM 87104

Salsa Express, PO Box 3985, Albuquerque, NM 87190

Seeds/Plants

Native Seed/SEARCH, 2509 N. Campbell Ave. #325, Tucson, AZ 85719

Pepper Gal, PO Box 23006, Fort Lauderdale, FL 33307

Plants of the Southwest, Rt. 6, Box 11A, Santa Fe, NM 87501

Redwood City Seed Company, PO Box 361, Redwood City, CA 94064

Seed Savers Exchange, PO Box 70, Decorah, IA 52101

Seeds of Change, PO Box 15700, Santa Fe, NM 87501

Shepherd's Garden Seeds, 30 Irene Street, Torrington, CT 06790

Talavaya Seeds, PO Box 707, Santa Cruz Station, Santa Cruz, NM 87567

Bibliography

Books

Andrews, Jean. *Peppers: The Domesticated Capsicums.* Austin: University of Texas Press, 1985.

————. *Red Hot Peppers.* New York: Macmillan, 1993.

Dent, Huntley. *The Feast of Santa Fe.* New York: Simon and Schuster, 1985.

DeWitt, Dave and Paul A. Bosland. *The Pepper Garden,* Berkeley, CA: Ten Speed Press, 1993.

DeWitt, Dave and Mary Jane Wilan. *The Food Lover's Handbook to the Southwest.* Rocklin, CA: Prima Press, 1992.

Dille, Carolyn and Susan Belsinger. *Classic Southwest Cooking.* Rocklin, CA: Prima Press, 1993.

Miller, Mark. *The Great Chile Book.* Berkeley, CA: Ten Speed Press, 1991.

Miller, Richard L. *The Official Fajita Cookbook.* Austin: Texas Monthly Press, 1988.

Naj, Amal. *Peppers: A Story of Hot Pursuits.* New York: Alfred A. Knopf, 1992.

Schweid, Richard. *Hot Peppers: Cajuns and Capsicum in New Iberia, Louisiana.* Berkeley, CA: Ten Speed Press, 1989.

Periodicals

Check, William. "Hot Peppers for Pain." *Reader's Digest,* June 1990, p. 107

Cotton, Paul. "Studying selective blockage of sensation." *Journal of the American Medical Association,* July 4, 1990, pp. 14–15.

Ezzell, Carol. "A Peppery Preventative for Pain." *Science News,* November 14, 1992, p. 333.

Gutfield, Greg, Melissa Meyers, and Maureen Sangiorgio. "Cool off pain with a pepper." *Prevention,* April, 1991, p. 12.

"Effect of treatment with cap-saicin on daily activities of patients with painful diabetic neuropathy." (Abstract), *Journal of the American Medical Association.* September, 23, 1992, P. 1524.

McCourt, Richard, "Some like it hot." *Discover.* August, 1991, p. 48.

"Not too hot to handle." *Tufts University Diet & Nutrition Letter.* May, 1992, p. 8.

Raloff, Janet. "Hot Prospects for quelling cluster headaches." *Science News,* July 13, 1991, p. 20.

"Chili Hot Chemistry." *Science News.* December 12, 1992, p. 404.

Papers

Hudgins, Sharon. "Powdered Chiles and Chili Powder". Paper presented at the Oxford Symposium on Food and Cookery. Oxford, England, 1992.

Hudgins, Tom. "Hot Sauces: Fiery Flavorings". Paper presented at the Oxford Symposium on Food and Cookery. Oxford, England, 1992.

INDEX

addictive power of chiles 15
Anaheims 28, 31, 33
anchos 19, **25**
Andrews, Jean 9
anthracnose 32, 33
aphids 32
Arawak, the 10, 14
Aztecs 9, 13

banana peppers 26, 28, 33
black pepper 10

Cajun spices 15
"Calicut" peppers 11
California chiles 26
capsaicin 15, 16, 18, 20
Capsicum 9
cayennes **13**, 24, 26, 27, 33
chart of chile varieties 34–37
cherry peppers 26, 28, 33
chile juice 15
chile, origin of word 10
chile, spelling of 10
chiles, see individual varieties
chiles, cooking 22 ff; cultivation of
    30; curative power of 18; dried
    21, 24, 26, 27; drying 27;
    fertilizing 29; for pain relief 18;
    global dispersion of 11; grinding
    27; growing 28 ff; harvesting
    31; history 9; mitigating the
    effects of 21; peeling 22; pests
    and diseases of 32; pickled 26;
    propagation of 28; pungency of
    20; roasting 22, 24; skinning
    22; toasting 24; vitamins in 19

chili powder, history of 14
chile molido 27
chiles de árbol **25**
chipotles 12, **25**, **26**
Columbus, Christopher 10
companion plants 33
cooking chiles 22
Creole spices 15
cross-pollination 30
cultivating chiles 30
curative power of chiles 18

de árbols 12, 24
Domenici, Sen. Pete 10
dried chiles 21, 24, 26, 27
drying chiles 27

effect of soil on chiles 20
endorphins 16, 18, 19

family of chiles 9
fertilizing chiles 29
Fresnos 24, 26, 33

Gebhardt, William 14
genus of chiles 9
global dispersion of chiles 11
grinding chiles 27
growing chiles 28 ff
guajillos 12

habaneros 12, **17**, 20, 24, **25**, 26,
    31, 33
harvesting chiles 31
herbs with chiles 33
history of chili powder 14

history of chiles 9 ff
hot hands 16

Incas 13
International Connoisseurs of
    Green and Red Chile, The 15

jalapeños **13**, 21, 24, 26, 28, 33
juice, of chiles 15

leaf spot 32, 33

Mayas 9, 13
McIlhenny family 14
mitigating the effects of chiles 21
mosaics 32
mulatos 22, 26, 33

Naj, Amal 16
New Mexico chiles 22, 26, 33
New Mexico reds **25**

origin of word chile 10
ornamental peppers **32**, 33

pain relief, chiles for 18
paprika 27
pasillas 19, 33
peeling chiles 22
Penderly, DeWitt Clinton 14
piquíns **13**, 24, 26, 33
Peppers: A Story of Hot Pursuits 16
pests and diseases of chiles 32
pickled chiles 26
Piper nigrum 10
poblanos 19, 22, 26, 28, 33

propagation of chiles 28
pungency 20

red pepper flakes 27
ristras 12, 26, 27
roasted chiles 24
roasting chiles 22
rocatillos **17**, 33
Rozin, Elizabeth 16
Rozin, Paul 16

Santa Fe Grandes 24, 26, 33
Scotch bonnets 12, **17**
Scoville Organoleptic Test 16
Scoville, Wilbur 16
serranos **13**, 20, 21, 33
skinning chiles 22
soil, for growing chiles 20, 30
Solanaceae 9
spelling of chile 10
Substance P 18
sweet bell peppers 22

Tabasco Pepper Sauce 14
tabascos **13**, 16, 21, **29**, 33
tepíns 21, 33
Thai peppers 12, **13**, 21, 24, 26, 33
toasting chiles 24
Tournefort 10

vanillyl amides 15
vitamins in chiles 19

RECIPE INDEX

**APPETIZERS AND
FIRST COURSES 39**
Yucatán Style Ceviche **39**, 40
Crab and Corn Soup with Chiles
    41
Fajita Taquitos 42
Garden-Style Guacamole Tostados
    44
Fresh Tuna and Serrano Salad 45
Pepper and Corn Pancakes 46

SAUCES 47
Red Chile Sauce **47**, 48
Roasted Chile and Herb Sauce 49
Green Chile Sauce **47**, 50
Walnut, Cayenne, and Coriander
    Sauce 52

MAIN DISHES 53
Carribean-Style Pork with Hot
    Frying Peppers **53**, 54
Jerk Chicken 56
Chile Con Carne 58
Sea Bass with Vegetables en
    Escabeche 59
White Bean Chile 60
Black Bean Chile 62
Chile Relleno Enchiladas 63
Eggs with Chiles and Tortillas 64
Vegetables and Salads 65
Fruit Salad with Chiles and Lime
    65, 66
Cabbage Chile Slaw 67

Spicy Noodle and Vegetable Salad
    68
Pico de Gallo 70
Potatoes Baked with Onions,
    Green Chiles, and Tomatoes 71
Rice and Roasted Corn and Pepper
    Salad 72

**SALSAS AND
ACCOMPANIMENTS 73**
Green Tomato Salsa **23**, **73**, 74
Habanero, Tomatillo, and Orange
    Salsa **23**, **73**, 75
Mango Salsa **23**, **73**, 76
Red Chile Salsa 77
Pantry Chipotle Salsa 78
Chipotle, Bean, and Sour Cream
    Dip 79
Vegetables en Escabeche 80
Green Chile Jelly **73**, 81
Hot and Sweet Pepper Relish 82
Hot Chile Oil or Vinegar 83
Pickled Peppers **73**, 84
Chile Powder **73**, 86

DESSERTS 87
Chocolate Chile Pecan Brownies
    87, 88
Holy Moly Ice Cream 90